SO-CBF-240

# Part-Time Careers

## For anyone who wants more than just a job—but less than a 40-hour week!

By
Joyce Hadley

CAREER PRESS
180 Fifth Avenue
P.O. Box 34
Hawthorne, NJ 07507
1-800-CAREER-1
201-427-0229 (outside U.S.)
FAX: 201-427-2037

Copyright © 1993 by Career Press

### PART-TIME CAREERS
**FOR ANYONE WHO WANTS MORE THAN JUST A JOB—
BUT LESS THAN A 40-HOUR WEEK!**
ISBN 1-56414-073-3, $10.95
Cover design by A Good Thing, Inc.
Printed in the U.S.A. by Book-mart Press

To order this title by mail, please include price as noted above, $2.50 handling per order, and $1.00 for each book ordered. Send to: Career Press, Inc., 180 Fifth Ave., P.O. Box 34, Hawthorne, NJ 07507

Or call toll-free 1-800-CAREER-1 (Canada: 201-427-0229) to order using VISA or MasterCard, or for further information on books from Career Press.

While much careful thought and depth of research have been devoted to the writing of this book, all content is to be viewed as general information only. The reader is urged to consult competent career professionals for details about any of the careers or work options addressed in this book, including specifics such as salary ranges, required training and education and future opportunities.

## Library of Congress Cataloging-in-Publication Data

Part-time careers : for anyone who wants more than just a job--
    but less than a 40-hour week! / by Career Press Inc.
        p. cm.
    ISBN 1-56414-073-3 : $10.95
    1. Part-time employment.  I. Career Press Inc.
HD5110.P37   1993
331.7'02--dc20                                        93-22400
                                                         CIP

# Acknowledgments

This book would never have been possible without the experiences of the women and men who are breaking new ground in their companies, building successful home-based businesses and following their dreams. Your willingness and eagerness to share your triumphs—and be just as candid about your trials—have enriched this book without measure.

I am also grateful to the many people inside companies on the cutting edge in the area of work/family programs and flexible work options for taking time to update me on your progress—especially Cathy Fowler at U S West, Inc.

Special thanks to Betsy Sheldon at Career Press, whose interest and enthusiasm for this subject added to my own and whose expert guidance and encouragement have greatly enhanced this book.

Stacy McMullen, Barbara Oertli, Martha Roberts, Suzanne Sherman, Linda Marks and Tara Grusin introduced me to many of the people whose stories appear here. Tracy Fetters understands the rigors of the writing life and, like me, wouldn't choose to live any other. Thank you all for your generous contributions and friendship.

And finally, to my mother and father, Nancy and Richard Hadley. My mother, a friend, supporter and devil's advocate—has somehow known exactly when to play each role. I hope I am capable of such grace one day. My father, who "reinvented" himself as a consultant after age 50, today "walks on water" according to his clients. I continue to be inspired by his example. Thanks to both of you for giving me wings, but always a place to come back to earth. This is for you.

# Contents

# Part 3
### New ways to work:
### Finding nontraditional career options in the corporate world

# Part 4
### Coming home:
### Creating a home-based business (and a more satisfying life)

# Part 5
### "Gotta dance:"
### Using part-time work to pursue a passion

# Part 1

# The part-time revolution: Benefiting from a new economic order

*"There is no security on this earth. There is only opportunity."*
—Douglas MacArthur

# Chapter 1

# Reengineering the American Dream

A new breed of dinosaur is lumbering toward certain extinction.

The American corporation, born in the Industrial Age and shaped for mass production, has ruled our economy for decades with a bigger-is-better ethic. Over the years, big gains and little competition made it easy for this giant to become arrogant—and grow complacent.

But like those massive and mighty creatures of eons ago, the American corporation has become increasingly vulnerable to a changing environment. Too many years of business-as-usual have made it plodding and unimaginative. New technology and increased competition from global markets require a leaner, swifter and more cunning animal. Changing social values and a more heterogeneous work force require a friendlier approach.

What may have been an appropriate structure to keep the immigrant employee population of the Industrial Age "in line" has already proven ludicrous in the current Age of Knowledge. In order for all of us to survive, the American corporation must be reborn.

## A world gone crazy

For most of us, that's a scary proposition. Over several generations, we've grown dependent on a corporate ethic that promises a "good job" and a secure future in exchange for our 40 or more hours a week. We've accepted business cycles and soldiered through recessions and downturns in the economy. But we've always returned to the status quo.

Lately, however, something more is going on. Large corporations that began downsizing in the '80s have continued to shed tens of thousands of jobs at a time. High-tech Microsoft, Inc., tiny in comparison to General Motors, slipped past that mammoth corporation in total stock market value early in 1992. And Manpower, Inc., the temporary services firm, is officially the nation's largest private-sector employer, with more than half a million "employees" on its roster.

In a world that seems to have gone crazy, "All that's left is to change everything," management guru Tom Peters told the readers of *Working Woman* magazine. Economic and industry experts agree. Not only are fundamental changes in the way we work long overdue—but they are not over by a long shot. Throughout the '90s, we can expect companies to continue to downsize and out-source work traditionally done by full-time employees to a growing legion of contractors and temporary workers.

## "Betrayal" or boon?

What has been called by some a betrayal of the American ethic, heralds a fundamental change in the relationship between companies and their employees. Painful, yes. But many feel the process will open new opportunities for both parties.

With the expedient measures not yet over, companies are already beginning to reshape and reengineer the workplace in ways that make sense for the age in which we live. More companies are answering employees' fears with straight talk about the certainty of more change and upheaval in the years ahead. Some companies and employees are already working as partners on task forces designed to streamline business processes.

The challenge for employees—those who are displaced as well as those who are left behind—will be to embrace a new sense of independence, what Tom Peters calls a "return to the true American ethic of Emersonian self-reliance."

## The inevitable evolution

In this brave new world of work, a rigid corporate hierarchy is likely to give way to a team ethic. "Company" men and women will be replaced by employee-entrepreneurs. Seniority will be the product of a self-directed career. And the root of our security will be in the "skills portfolios" we carry.

**The small shall inherit the market.** Big companies are breaking apart into more manageable networked teams and groups. Many are trimming down to "core competencies," those operations at the heart of the business, and parceling out remaining functions to contractors and temporaries.

Experts such as Tom Peters predict that a series of small, multi-disciplinary project teams may eventually replace more traditional functional groups in many companies—bringing an entrepreneurial energy to the halls of big business.

**A small company with big-company style.** Donna Wotton is one small business owner who finds she can run her small event-planning business like a big company, using a team approach. With three people under her own roof, she "recruits" team players from a network of other self-employed people and small businesses, mixing and matching talent as the projects require. "We meet as a team with the client as if we were one company," she says. "We work together fairly regularly as a group, so we know each other's working styles and really enjoy working together. If we're overload, we just bring in another coordinator. Clients get really top-notch talent for exactly what they need, rather than having to keep these people on staff."

**Turning the pyramid on its ear.** Nordstrom set the pace for other companies weighed down by a bottom-heavy organization chart. The retailer simply turned it upside down. By placing its sales force at the top the chart and giving it the power to make decisions that would result in better service to customers, the company was able to increase sales from $769 million to $3.4 billion over the last 10 years.

## Changing values

Meanwhile, the work force is changing, too. For a growing number of maturing baby boomers, the 60-hour work week has begun to lose its allure. The siren song of "Do what you love" is luring more people to take time out to pursue personal interests and prompting mothers and fathers to spend more time raising a family.

**"There must be more to life..."** A year ago, Donna Wotton convinced her friend Nancy to quit her job. "She'd been an advertising sales rep for a big trade publisher for 10 years. She made a bundle of money, spent it hand over fist and then lived hand-to-mouth. She finally asked herself 'Why am I doing this? I don't care about electronics,' " Donna says.

So she quit her job and eventually moved to San Francisco where she plans to work in the nonprofit sector pursuing a long time interest—women's issues. "When she first came out here, she was so angry," Donna remembers. "This was not the Nancy that I knew. Now she looks five years younger than she did three months ago. All the things that are important to her, she's put back in her life."

# Part-Time Careers

**A retiring market.** At the beginning of the century, senior citizens accounted for a modest sliver of the population—about 13 percent. For most, the "twilight years" were spent far away from the world of work. Even as late as 1960, only about 6 percent of the retirement population expressed interest in continuing to work.

But times are changing. Today, senior citizens are a healthy, active group, unwilling—and often economically unable—to retire full-time to the golf course. Many choose to remain active as consultants or work part-time to supplement Social Security, savings and other investment income. By the time baby boomers reach retirement age, this "senior segment" is expected to represent a more sizable wedge of the population (21 percent) and the part-time work force.

**Women: The flexibility leaders.** Also present in record number are women. In 1992, women comprised 57.8 percent of the U.S. labor force. And currently, 41 percent of all managers are women. Whether they are partners in two-income families or single parents, working women are a group with the clout to serve up family issues on the corporate agenda.

The landmark Family and Medical Leave Act was a step in the right direction. While it assures workers in companies with more than 50 employees the right to take up to 12 weeks of unpaid, job-protected leave for the birth of a child, an adoption, a serious illness or to care for a seriously ill family member, many employees may not be able to afford to go that long without a paycheck. Many more employees work for small businesses not covered by the Act or are self-employed.

## The part-time solution

Part-time work is becoming a viable option for many people—parents and others looking for more balance between work and personal life.

According to "Working Options," the newsletter of the Association of Part-Time Professionals, more than 4.5 million of the approximately 20 million people now working part-time are professionals. Most are engineers, math and computer scientists, natural scientists, health care specialists, university, college and other teachers, and lawyers and judges—90 percent of whom work part-time by choice.

For companies, part-time work and flexible work options offer another opportunity to trim expenses (related to benefits and overhead) while retaining the expertise of new mothers and retirees. Some companies proudly publicize their work/family policies in order to attract the best new recruits from a dwindling labor pool.

A 1990 survey of 521 large companies by the Conference Board, a business research group based in New York City, found that 90 percent of the employers claimed to offer part-time schedules, and 50 percent said they offered flextime.

**Lifestyle or luxury?** But is working part-time a luxury only a few can afford? Certainly, some groups will find it easier to take advantage of part-time options—primarily women who are partners in two-income households.

Still many of these families must decide to get by on less for a temporary or extended period. But "getting by," even for a short time, may affect long-term savings for college and retirement. Two-income families may also find it easier to consolidate health care benefits coverage under one spouse's employer.

Benefits can be a major issue for some families. By federal law, employers must make Social Security contributions and open pension plans for employees and temporaries who work more than 1,000 hours a year.

According to the 1992 Employee Benefits Report, issued by the U.S. Chamber of Commerce, the number of firms offering full benefits to part-time employees increased by 15 percent over the previous year. But the report notes that benefits policies still vary considerably by industry and by firm.

In its "Personnel Policies Forum," the Bureau of National Affairs reports nearly 50 percent of the organizations responding provide health care coverage to employees who work at least 17.5 hours per week, 37 percent offer dental insurance and 20 percent offer long-term disability plans.

Organizations with a large number of part-time employees—hospitals and banks, for example—are more likely to court part-timers with special benefits packages. But most companies continue to prorate coverage. So, potential part-timers need to become familiar with the benefits policies at their own firms before proposing an arrangement they won't be able to afford.

What about men? Some companies—and some men—are slow to yield. There may a cultural "taboo" discouraging parental leaves or flexible arrangements for men, or employees may feel they have to "play it safe" to hang onto their jobs.

**The temporary connection.** Many displaced workers, more and more of them professionals, are turning to another part-time option—temporary work. In fact, 1.5 million temps go to work each day for companies nationwide. They may stay a day, but more often it is a week or a couple of months.

They are secretaries, yes, but also bailiffs and lawyers, loan officers and engineers. Many plan to continue living the "temporary" lifestyle—picking up assignments as necessary—to escape stress, politics and long hours. One Connecticut-based firm specializes in providing senior executives who are expert at turnarounds.

As companies continue to practice "accordion management," expanding and contracting their work force according to business needs, temporary workers, often paid high hourly rates, will continue to be in demand. In fact, since 1982, temporary employment has increased almost 250 percent, while all other employment has grown less than 20 percent.

Diane Thrailkill advises the people who attend her seminars on temporary work to think of themselves as owners of small businesses.

Whatever their history, whatever their goals, she encourages her audiences to make their skills their medium of exchange. "I tell people that if you're going to be successful at temping, you have to have a skills-based mentality," she says. "You are in charge of selling your time and your talent by the hour. Your time is money."

**The entrepreneurial employee.** Increasingly, we will become a work force made up of "skills merchants." Companies and jobs no longer offer longevity. Skills ensure security and satisfaction and mobility. They are the tools of your trade. Finish up a job or short-term project, pack up and move on to the next job, project or even industry. On the way, you'll need to sharpen your skills and take responsibility for adding new ones to your repertoire whenever possible.

**The big four.** A combination of specialized knowledge and technical skills will sustain most professionals in this new age. For example, a public relations pro should be proficient at desktop publishing. A health care professional may want to learn Spanish. Experts agree that professionals should focus on acquiring and sharpening skills in these four key areas in the '90s:

- Computer literacy
- Written communication
- Public and presentation speaking
- Foreign language

**A return to self-reliance.** Back in 1970, only 7 percent of the population was self-employed. In 1990, 50 percent of us were on our own, and the number is rising. Women frustrated by corporate politics and stymied by a "glass ceiling" continue to find independence and satisfaction as small business owners. Businesses owned by women today employ more Americans than Fortune 500 companies!

Now the market is opening up to a new cadre of displaced workers and would-be entrepreneurs who'll begin new careers as consultants and home-based business owners in the '90s.

## Replacing fear with power

What about you? If you're ready to take charge of your professional destiny—by working part-time, telecommuting or sharing a job within your company—the time has never been so ripe to make the change. Let's take a closer look at the many options you can choose from as you begin to forge a new part-time career.

# Chapter 2

# Just what is a part-time career?

Anybody can work part-time. In fact, almost everybody has at one time or another—an after-school job at a fast-food place, a summer stint as a lifeguard, an evening commitment of tutoring after your *real* job. But you may have always believed that once you entered a profession and started to build a career, there was an unspoken covenant: Thou shalt work full-time, or thou wilt not get ahead.

Thankfully, things are changing. These days, you can continue to build your career while working 20 or 30 hours a week. You can work a home-based business in as few as 15. You can drop in and out as a telecommuter or just take on projects. You can use part-time or temporary work to buy time to work on a personal project. Even if you find yourself closing in on full-time, there are a number of ways you can "flex" your hours to fit the lifestyle you choose.

What will you sacrifice? Of course, you'll give up some of your salary and many, if not all, of your benefits to work fewer hours. But you'll also give up stress that can leave you burned out if you're trying to "do it all."

# Part-Time Careers

However, believe it or not, you don't have to sacrifice status or interesting work or career advancement. In the chapters that follow, you'll learn how to negotiate the right part-time career for you.

## Choose a workstyle to suit your lifestyle

For the purposes of this book, we'll broaden the definition of "part-time" far beyond the traditional borders of punching the corporate time clock for 30 hours or fewer a week. Part-time, for our purposes, will expand to include other flexible work options, including:

**Regular part-time work** (also referred to as working *shortened hours* or a *shortened work week*). Some companies and businesses traditionally offer part-time hours that may be rigid—every weekday from noon to 4 p.m., for example. But more and more, if you work from 20 to 30 hours a week, you may be able to choose any combination of days and hours, such as three eight-hour days or two 10-hour days.

**Job-sharing.** As part of a job-sharing team, you'll work part-time to carry out the tasks and responsibilities of one position that demands full-time coverage. You and your partner may work an equal number of hours on different days to cover the standard work week, or one partner may opt to work longer hours. There is typically a certain amount of overlapping time scheduled to encourage communication between the job-sharing partners. Many job-sharers hold management-level jobs. Some are supervisors. All can be promoted.

**Telecommuting** (sometimes called *flexplace* or *work-from-home*). You may spend all of your time working from home or at a satellite office. Or you may choose to stay home to work on a project or work longer, or "odd," hours. While many people can work from home with a telephone and personal computer, you may need to be connected to the company's computer and electronic mail system. Some companies allow employees to borrow laptop computers to work at home or while traveling.

**Temporary work.** By registering with one or more temporary services agencies, you can be called to "fill in" at many different companies for a day, a week or several months. Temporaries typically don't receive benefits. Those who work 1,000 hours (about five months) for a company may become eligible to receive health care coverage.

Professionals, such as accountants and lawyers, as well as people with extensive computer experience are often paid high hourly rates.

Some companies manage an internal pool of temporary employees who are always "on call."

**Independent contractors/consultants/freelancers.** If you are self-employed and working out of your home on a contract or project basis, you often have some leeway in setting your fees and hours. Contract workers may have to work full-time or *more* than full-time on the company premises while completing a project. In this feast-or-famine business, intense periods of work may be followed by "slow" periods of little or no work.

**Phased or partial retirement.** A gradual shift from full-time to retirement may be an option for older workers, who can reduce their hours for a period of time prior to retiring full-time. Phased retirement programs generally define a timeline to retirement. Partial retirement may or may not allow senior employees to draw partial retirement benefits and has no set time limit.

## Choose a schedule to suit your needs

**By the week.** Work three regular 9-to-5 days as a part-timer. Or two and a half days a week as part of a job-sharing team. Or one or two days here and there as a professional

19

temporary. Or seven days in 10, with every Friday and every other Monday off.

**By the hour.** You may take a two-hour lunch to teach a yoga class. Or shave the last two hours off the day to meet the school bus. You may begin working in your bathrobe at 5:30 a.m. Or, as a freelancer, you may end up working weekends to meet a deadline and treat yourself to a Monday matinee.

**By the project.** Your work may require an intense schedule for three months, then you switch back to your part-time schedule or job-sharing arrangement when the project is completed. Or you might work day and night to fill an order as a home-based business owner and take the next week off when business is slow.

**By the season.** You may be able to arrange to work fewer hours, or not work at all, in the summer. Or you might take on project work that has you working for three months with the next three months off.

**By your whim.** Change work schedules by the week or the season as your needs demand by working out an informal trial arrangement with your supervisor. Or you may be able to decide to work from home at the last minute on a Tuesday morning. As a temp, you can pick and choose your assignments that can range from a day to several weeks or months.

## Flexible options for full-time workers

Depending on your needs, you may be able to use one or more of these flexible arrangements to free up time at odd hours or on certain days of the week.

**Flextime.** You choose when you start work and when you quit each day within the limits set by management. Usually, a company will designate a "band" of two or three flexible hours at either end of a "core" period of the day, during which all employees must be present (9 a.m. to 3 p.m., for example.) Some companies offer flexibility around the noon hour.

You may choose to arrive at work later one or two days a week for personal reasons. Or work shorter days. Or you may ask for a consistent schedule that lies slightly outside of the typical 9-to-5, such as 7:30 a.m. to 3:30 p.m.

**Extended work week.** You may work fewer hours a day, but stretch those hours over as many as six days per week.

**Compressed work week.** If you work full-time, you may opt to work longer and fewer days per week. A typical compressed work week consists of four 10-hour days. A common variation is a two-week schedule made up of five nine-hour days followed by a week of four nine-hour days.

**Paid leave.** Some companies allow employees time off to care for a sick child, as well as for vacations and sabbaticals. Time off for new mothers generally falls under the company's disability leave policy. Some companies encourage sabbaticals for employees in middle and upper-management.

**Unpaid leave.** Many companies allow employees to take an unpaid leave of absence from work to complete community service work, pursue an education, care for a dependent family member or newborn. The Family and Medical Leave Act affects companies with more than 50 employees and permits up to 12 weeks of unpaid leave for men and women who must stay home for a number of reasons.

But policies can vary dramatically from company to company. If you're considering taking an unpaid leave, it pays to know how long you can be away and whether you will retain your job, benefits coverage and seniority.

If you didn't find your option here, you may be able to design your own. But first, meet some people who have forged exciting new work options for themselves.

# Chapter 3

# Is a part-time career right for you?

Your personal values and your goals will dictate whether a part-time career is right for you. For example, can you afford to trade part of your salary and benefits for more time to spend with your children or pursuing a personal interest? Can your job be done in less time—without costing you status? Have you built up enough goodwill to be able to propose something like this to your manager?

In the chapters that follow, you'll have the opportunity to explore many part-time options. There'll be plenty of issues and questions that will jog your thinking. But for now, the following exercise is designed to help you think more creatively about your individual situation. So, be honest. And be bold. Borrow ideas from the people here. Remember, you are in control of your career. So take your first step.

## 1. Who are you?

Your age doesn't matter. But your gender might. Your geographical location is not important. (Unless you plan to change it and want to work out a flexible arrangement to accommodate a move.)

Part-time work and flexible work arrangements appeal most to people who are—temporarily or permanently—looking for more balance between work and other interests. You may be considering part-time work if you are now—or expect to be:

- ❑ A new mother or father.
- ❑ A parent involved in family and/or school activities.
- ❑ A retiree.
- ❑ A freelancer or owner of a home-based business.
- ❑ An aspiring novelist, artist or singer, or are passionately pursuing some other interest.
- ❑ Unemployed or changing professions.
- ❑ A full-time homemaker ready to reenter the work force.
- ❑ Other _____

## 2. What are your goals?

Are you overwhelmed by the task of caring for your newborn? Are you finishing a novel or finishing school? Planning to start a home-based business? Your goals will determine the kind of flexibility you'll need. You attention is likely to be focused in one of these three areas:

### Family interests
- ❑ You want to spend more time with a new baby.
- ❑ Your kids are out of diapers, but you want to attend their school events and watch them grow up.
- ❑ You need more time off to care for a sick family member.

"I don't think I would happy being home all the time with three 'screamin' meemies' all around me," admits Beverly Dinan. But since the birth of her son 10 years ago, followed by twins a year and a half later, she's negotiated a variety of part-time schedules. During her time off, she stays in touch, picking up her electronic mail via her home computer and answering the occasional phone call.

"I put in over 140 hours of volunteer time last year," says Larry Nash. For the past three years, telecommuting has made it possible for him to flex his hours around classroom activities and school board meetings on a regular basis. In fact, he is such a common visitor to his daughter's classroom that her friends have asked, "What kind of job does your dad have?" He says, "Sometimes I work at home in the evening or come into work early in the morning. I have a very understanding boss who encourages my involvement."

## Personal interests
❑ You want to return to school.
❑ You want to free up more time to pursue an interest or special project—or you simply want more leisure time.
❑ You're planning to retire and want—or need—to continue working.
❑ You want more time to do volunteer work.

"I want the mindless stuff. I don't want it to take anything from me," says Diane Thrailkill, an author, seminar leader and self-proclaimed professional temp for the past six years. As a former trainer, her computer skills bring her a higher-than-average hourly wage. And her self-discipline on the job buys her from two to four hours a day to work on her own writing projects. "I have a different agenda than a lot of people. I don't want to socialize. I want to do their work as quickly and efficiently as possible—and then do my own work. That allows me to be very productive, which makes me happy," she admits.

Trish Adams has been waiting 20 years to complete her degree. After raising a family and developing a career, she has become a home-based business person and a part-time student. "I need four units to get my degree. I probably work my

Mary Kay Cosmetics business 10 to 15 hours a week so I've got plenty of time now."

Although she's been successfully balancing nursing and freelance photography for the past 14 years, "Right now, my goals have shifted," says Eleanor Bissell. "I can see my way clear to an early retirement, so now I don't mind putting in more hours at the hospital and maxing out on the savings, knowing that I'll be having so much more freedom, so much more time."

## Career/business interests

- ❑ You want to start a home-based business, or supplement the income you already have.
- ❑ You want to change professions and need time off to explore the options.
- ❑ You've taken time off to raise a family full-time and you'd like to start back to work part-time.
- ❑ You've been laid off and are looking for a full-time job.
- ❑ You're planning to move and want to continue working for the same company.

When she found herself unable to concentrate on anything but her jewelry creations, "It was time to make the jump," says Diane Hyde. She landed on both feet, running her own home-based business. She quickly discovered that it was one thing to run a booming business from her office during the Christmas season, and quite another to purchase jewelry components, maintain inventory, price and market her growing line of jewelry at art shows, in department stores and through catalogs. "You have to be ready to fail, or you'll never try," she says. "And you'll never know if you could have succeeded."

Mary Lou Sweeney has a plan. "I'm going to make myself invaluable," she says. While her accounting department has undergone a reorganization and prepares to go "live" with a new computer system, she is sopping up as much knowledge as she can, and keeping her ears open. Job security is just one of her motives. At the age of 61, she is also hoping to negotiate a telecommuting arrangement that will allow her to begin an early working-retirement from her new home in Sequim on Washington's Olympic Peninsula. "I really like my job," Mary Lou says. "There's no reason I can't continue to be a member of this department and do it from Sequim."

### 3. What are your skills?

Once you realize you are in the business of marketing your expertise, you can begin to think less in terms of your job description and more about the "package" of skills you can "sell" your company—skills that your management should find difficult to part with.

As you fine-tune your professional portfolio, think about whether you could use a flexible arrangement to enhance what you can offer. For example, if you do a lot of writing, telecommuting would help you do more work, free from interruptions. If you have a customer-intensive situation, sharing your job with another person will give clients more than full-time coverage. (If you can't think of anything, don't worry. The following chapters offer detailed information that will stimulate your thinking.)

**Identify your professional "skills portfolio."** Like stock, your stock and trade becomes more valuable with each passing year. List the skills you've been paid for, as well as those you've developed by pursuing a hobby or doing volunteer work. Don't forget to include those things that other people have told you you're great at doing.

Your skills portfolio will include generic, but concrete descriptions of specific tasks and accomplishments that include words like "managed," "analyzed," "created" and "produced." Use these to develop a skills-based resume. Rather than think of yourself as a public relations manager for a leading software company, recast yourself as a communications-and-marketing professional specializing in consumer product introductions.

If you plan on starting a home-base business, this list will help you see the "holes" in your knowledge. You'll have to learn what you need to know, or hire someone else to fill in the gaps. You'll also have to work hard to stay up-to-date on all the skills at the heart of your business.

**Identify yourself as the entrepreneur who will sell it.** By now you know you're on your own, even if you stay with a company. That means you'll continue to sell yourself and develop your career as long as you work anywhere.

Self-discipline, self-confidence, self-motivation. These are just a few the "self" skills you'll need to develop and polish. As an entrepreneur you'll also need to be:

- ❏ Personable
- ❏ Flexible
- ❏ Motivating
- ❏ Supportive
- ❏ Responsible

- ❏ A consistent performer
- ❏ Detailed-oriented
- ❏ Organized
- ❏ Innovative
- ❏ Comfortable with change

Your personal and professional skills should be the source of your security. If not, "relocate" your sense of security in yourself. If your security comes from your job or your company, or anywhere else outside yourself, you will always be vulnerable to change.

## 4. What are you afraid of?

Now, we're down to the nitty-gritty. What keeps you awake at night thinking about what could go wrong?

# Part-Time Careers

**"I'll end up on a 'mommy track.'"** You may, if you don't have a plan that covers you from getting your part-time arrangement approved through future promotions. You'll find more detailed information on drafting a proposal in Chapter 9.

Once you're on the job, compensate for the disadvantages of working fewer hours, such as not being around as much, by communicating more with managers and co-workers using electronic mail updates, memos and brief phone messages.

And play up the advantages. For example, your energy level will be higher than it would if you were trying to "do it all," so use it to be more productive.

Many women have been able to work fewer hours for several years without dealing a death blow to their future prospects. Set your own professional goals and ask for the responsibility, promotions and raises you feel you deserve.

The key is to manage your career at every stage—no matter what kind of schedule you work.

**"I'll feel guilty about not being a full-time mom."** Not every woman was cut out to be a full-time mom. Motherhood doesn't have to be an all-or-nothing proposition.

But if you were raised on milk and cookies in the '50s and '60s by a full-time mom, that may still be hard to swallow. Begin by fast-forwarding to the '90s. Your children are growing up in a world that values working women of all varieties. If your attitude is positive and upbeat and you attend special events and show an interest in their school work, they'll have a positive attitude about you as a working mom.

**"My boss will never approve."** You won't know that until you ask. In Part 3, you'll hear from people who have proposed flexible arrangements and gotten approval. You'll also try your hand at drafting a proposal and get tips for answering some of the objections your manager might raise. Companies are becoming more flexible. Even if you're turned down once, a reorganization or new manager can change everything.

**"It won't work out."** The important thing is to do your homework ahead of time. If you've asked for a trial period, you can use that time to fine-tune what isn't working. Maybe you've taken on too much work for the hours you're working and can share it with someone else. Maybe you've taken on the wrong job-share partner. If it doesn't work out, identify the problem and try again.

If you're a home-based business owner, your success will depend heavily on the time you spend on your business plan as well as the innovative methods you use to market your business.

**"I'll have to give up status and promotion."** Don't, if you can help it. Many managers spend a great deal of time away from the office, traveling or attending meetings. A number of managers have found that working from a remote location is not much different. Karen Dowell manages a staff of 14 in California working from her home office on an island off the coast of Maine. Lynn Winter Gross and Rose Krupp-Ayala share the job of director of public affairs for the Los Angeles Chapter of the American Diabetes Association.

## What are you waiting for?

With this general self-profile in hand, it's time to get down to work. In the pages that follow, you'll meet people who have managed to create some very unique workstyles. Use their success strategies to chart your own path. You haven't got a moment to lose.

# Part 2

# Working on change: The best prospects for part-time careers in the '90s—and beyond

*"The world is moving so fast these days that the (person) who says it can't be done is generally interrupted by someone who is doing it."*
—Harry Emerson Fosdick

# Chapter 4

# Tuning into
# the trends

Who wouldn't want a crystal ball these days? In what is commonly referred to as a "changing business climate," the only thing that is certain is that nothing is certain.

Technology has roared into every corner of the workplace—fundamentally changing the way we perform our jobs and spawning a new generation of home-based professionals.

Giants of industry are stooping, like Gulliver, to compete with a community of small businesses that are far more agile when responding to change. Some industries will wither in the decade ahead. Others, forged by technological advances, promise to become major players.

Add global markets, shifting social preferences and a population that is aging. Sprinkle liberally with new government legislation—and we're left with a complex stew that promises to change its flavor in unpredictable ways with each passing year.

The last generation to enjoy some semblance of stability will retire in this decade. In the years ahead, we'll all be challenged to take a broader view of opportunity. It will be abundant, but it will shift with the rapidly changing times. So where does that leave you in planning your part-time career?

The closest thing to a crystal ball may be the *Occupational Outlook Handbook* published every two years by the U.S. Department of Labor's Bureau of Labor Statistics. On the pages of this comprehensive resource, government soothsayers use data on current economic growth, industry output and emerging trends in employment by industry and occupation to forecast business and employment conditions for the next 15 years.

The picture is far from bleak. In this section, you'll read about 45 of the hottest prospects for part-time work. Not only will these jobs be in great demand throughout the '90s, but many of them promise a vast number of new openings. First, let's take a look at some trends that are driving change.

## 1. Education and training: It's what you know

In 1987, 45 percent of all employed workers had better than a high school education. By the year 2000, that number is expected to be up to 54 percent. College-educated professionals working in a range of industries will ride the crest of the wave of future employment. Even employers who didn't require a college degree a few years ago will begin to give preference to candidates with higher education or graduates of hands-on training through accredited programs.

But your education shouldn't end there. Once, you just needed the sheepskin to get a foot in the door of your first job. Those days are gone. Even workers in secure industries will be challenged regularly to learn new techniques and adapt to technological innovations. Many growing industries, such as health care, also require professionals to take licensing exams and stay abreast of changes through continuing education. Those who pursue voluntary certification can expect to stay a step ahead of the competition.

# Part-Time Careers

**Part-time strategy:** Invest in the most comprehensive education or training program available before entering a new industry. If you're working full-time, establish professional credentials and certification—especially if you're in a competitive industry. If you're a consultant, go the extra mile to establish and maintain voluntary credentials, and pursue continuing education to enhance your opportunities.

## 2. Generalization means greater marketability

Technology makes it tempting to specialize. But workers who have their sights set on management-level jobs or self-employment will need a range of technical, academic and business skills.

Although companies tend to take on people with specialized training as new hires, employers will increasingly value well-rounded middle and upper managers—professionals with business acumen, a track record for creative problem-solving and plenty of experience working with people.

**Part-time strategy:** Smaller companies tend to offer the best general experience to workers who are interested in developing a range of skills and hands-on experience. Rather than focusing on one specific area, you'll be encouraged to wear a variety of hats.

## 3. Demographics: The maturing of the workplace

Demographic studies provide solid clues to ways in which the marketplace is changing. Throughout the '90s, the general population will grow more slowly—and grow older. More baby boomers will enter middle age and more people will survive past the age of 85.

Demographics affect conditions in the work force as well. The number of young people entering the job market will decline—reflecting the baby "bust" of the '70s. One estimate indicates a shortfall of 23 million workers by the early '90s.

This should substantially sweeten opportunities for mature, experienced professionals and managers. By the year 2005, workers between the ages of 45 and 54 will account for 24 percent of the labor force, up 16 percent from 1990. Baby boomers will remain in the work force longer than any previous generation. By 2005, 15 percent of the labor force will be 55 or over—up from 12 percent in 1990.

The population over the age of 85 will grow more than three times as fast as the total population in the years between 1990 and 2005, significantly increasing the demand for health services.

**Part-time strategies:** Take a serious look at the health care professions if you're in the process of choosing a career. If you're a professional in or approaching the "mature," 45 to 54 age group, look for ways to market your professional experience as a teacher, trainer or consultant.

## 4. Women: Major players and lifestyle leaders

As women continue to build a strong presence in the work force, they will gain clout in a number of areas. Increased visibility should bring more equitable pay as well as new attention to family issues.

More women who are pursuing careers as members of two-income families will push for benefits such as childcare and more flexible work arrangements.

Many women who are stymied by glass ceilings and lack of flexibility in the workplace will go it alone. Today, 6 million businesses are owned by women. The success rate for women-owned business—75 percent compared to only 20 percent for all businesses—should encourage growth in this area.

**Part-time strategies:** Companies reluctant to sacrifice the expertise of professional women who might otherwise not return from maternity leave are becoming more open to experimenting with flexible work arrangements, such as part-time work and job-sharing. Resources for women who opt to start a business are more abundant then ever before.

## 5. Small businesses: Less is more

Since 1980, Fortune 500 companies have cut about 3.5 million jobs from their payrolls. A growing number of small businesses have added 20 million. Companies with fewer than 100 employees will generate up to half of new jobs in the '90s.

**Part-time strategy:** Smaller companies, especially new start-ups, are often less formal and more innovative when it comes to creating flexible working arrangements, such as telecommuting, for employees. Those with limited internal resources will continue to rely on the outside services provided by a range of self-employed contractors and consultants.

## 6. Geography: Mobility matters

Where you live can make a significant difference in how much you earn and how far you progress in your chosen career. Key areas of the country, such as Texas and California, will be rich with opportunities for technology professionals. Urban areas, such as New York and Los Angeles, promise more jobs and more opportunities for advancement for some occupations—such as publishing, acting and fashion design.

There are also clues that a major migration is underway. One *Time* magazine cover story reported that the Rocky Mountain states are welcoming more professionals and families who are tired of the hassle and high cost of living that plague many business "meccas" like Silicon Valley in California. Other popular alternatives are Santa Fe and Seattle.

**Part-time strategy:** Some of the least glamorous areas are ripe with opportunities for entrepreneurs and telecommuters. If you're single and footloose, ready to put down family roots or approaching retirement, you might take some time to consider moving to an area that will be most beneficial to your lifestyle and building a career by telecommuting or starting a home-based business.

Even the best projections are only good guesses. Whether you plan to find a new part-time job, negotiate a flexible working arrangement with your current employer or start your own business, your success will depend on your vigilance. If you're on the lookout for shifting blue skies, you're less likely to encounter surprises from out of the blue.

# Chapter 5

# Changes in industry, changes in occupations

We are now a nation focused on service.

Although construction and renovation of homes and commercial buildings should remain steady throughout the '90s, the growth of most goods-producing industries peaked in the late 1970s. Current projections indicate that a whopping 23 million of the 24.6 million new jobs expected to be created by 2005 will be in service-related industries.

Services in the areas of health care and business will lead the economy—although there should also be dynamic growth in education, social and legal services. Employment in these areas is expected to increase 38 percent—from 4.2 million to 5.8 million jobs by 2005. Among the hottest prospects: paralegals, health-care technicians and technologists, and computer programmers.

Self-employment will continue to be a major trend, especially among managers, administrators and executives who have been laid off or face early retirement. By 2005, nearly half a million jobs are expected to be created by people who start their own businesses. Home-based businesses providing a range of personal services to two-income families promise to do well throughout the '90s.

Here's a brief overview of what's hot:

## Health care: Taking care of an aging population

Improvements in medical technology and an aging population promise to make this the fastest-growing industry in the economy.

New opportunities for employment will spring up in an increasing number of outpatient facilities and in-home providers of short-term care for baby boomers who are moving into middle age, patients released early from hospitals and the elderly. Nursing homes will serve the long-term needs of a growing population over the age of 85.

**Good news for part-timers:** Health care has traditionally been a leader in providing part-time employment and flexible hours.

**The bottom line:** Employment is projected to grow from 8.9 million to 12.8 million jobs by 2005.

## Business services: Serving a changing work force

Advances in technology, a continuing trend toward office and factory automation and an increasing demand for specialized services—such as computer and data processing consulting—in private firms and government agencies will bring this industry to the forefront in the '90s.

**Good news for part-timers:** Firms that supply personnel—especially temporary help—are expected to see the most dynamic growth.

**The bottom line:** Employment is expected to grow from 5.2 million to 7.6 million jobs by 2005.

# Part-Time Careers

## Education: Teaching a more diverse population

Enrollment of the school-age children of baby boomers who have waited longer to have families is already on the rise. Older, foreign and part-time students also will find their ways to class, making prospects bright not only for teachers, but for counselors and administrative staff.

**Good news for part-timers:** Adult education and corporate training will become major growth areas as the '90s unfold, opening up additional opportunities for self-employed workers seeking part-time, seasonal or flexible hours.

**The bottom line:** Employment in public and private schools is expected to grow from 9.4 million to 16.7 million jobs by 2005.

## Social services: Caring for a changing nation

More residential care institutions will provide around-the-clock assistance to the elderly and others who are too ill or disabled to care for themselves. There will also be an increasing need for family services.

**Good news for part-timers:** Childcare and eldercare, traditionally areas that allow flexible hours, will expand rapidly.

**The bottom line:** Employment is expected to grow from 1.8 million to 2.9 million jobs by 2005.

## Retail: More money to spend

More money in our pockets and more women in the work force will mean more jobs for retail sales people—especially in apparel and accessory stores. Workers in restaurants will also benefit from significant growth.

**Good news for part-timers:** Retail stores and restaurants have traditionally offered part-time employment and flexible hours to workers of all ages.

**The bottom line:** Employment opportunities are expected to grow from 19.7 to 24.8 million jobs in 2005.

The following industries will show more modest growth of less than 25 percent in the next decade:

- **Real estate.** Although this area is very sensitive to unpredictable swings and cycles in the economy, rising income levels and new construction of housing will spur some growth.

- **Transportation.** Deregulation in the transportation industry has opened up new options for personal and business travel, and will continue to spur employment growth in the passenger transportation arrangement industry, which includes travel agencies.

- **Communications.** Many more communications professionals are opting for self-employment. Public relations specialists should enjoy the bright prospects— especially those with expertise in the areas of environmental concerns, biotechnology and law.

- **Government.** Employment in state and local government (excluding public education and public hospitals) should grow modestly. However, employment in federal government is expected to decline.

- **Agriculture.** Like construction, this is one of the few bright spots among goods-producing industries. It promises growth in areas related to services for businesses and two-income families, such as gardening and lawn care.

## The Top 45 Occupations

### Service industries

**Health care**
Dental Assistant
Dental Hygienist
EEG Technologist
Homemaker-Home Health Aide
Licensed Practical Nurse
Medical Records Technician
Nuclear Medicine Technologist
Occupational Therapist
Ophthalmic Laboratory
  Technician
Physical Therapist
Physician's Assistant
Psychologist
Radiologic Technologist
Recreation Therapist
Registered Nurse
Respiratory Therapist
Speech-Language
  Pathologist/Audiologist
Surgical Technologist

**Business services**
Accountant
Computer Programmer
Employment Interviewer
Management Consultant
Paralegal
Receptionist
Service Sales Representative

**Social services**
Preschool Worker
Social Worker

**Education**
Adult Education Teacher
Teacher's Aide

**Retail**
Retail Salesperson

**Personal**
Automotive Mechanic
Cosmetologist

**Real estate**
Real Estate Agent/Broker

**Transportation**
Flight Attendant
Reservation and Transportation
  Ticket Clerk
Travel Agent

**Communications/The Arts**
Actor/Dancer
Designer
Photographer
Public Relations Specialist
Fine Artist
Writer/Editor

### Goods-producing industries

**Construction**
Carpenter
Contractor

**Agriculture**
Gardener/Groundskeeper

## Top fastest-growing occupations

| | |
|---|---|
| Paralegal | Psychologist |
| Homemaker-Home Health Aide | Travel Agent |
| Physical Therapist | Flight Attendant |
| Radiologic Technologist | Computer Programmer |

## Top 10 largest job-growth occupations

| | |
|---|---|
| Retail Salesperson | Gardener and Groundskeepers |
| Registered Nurse | Accountant |
| Teacher | Computer Programmer |
| Receptionist | Teacher Aide |
| Preschool Worker | Licensed Practical Nurse |

## Fastest-growing occupations requiring degrees

| | |
|---|---|
| Physical Therapist | Teacher |
| Psychologist | Recreation Therapist |
| Computer Programmer | Accountant |
| Occupational Therapist | Social Worker |
| Public Relations Specialist | |

## Fastest-growing occupations requiring training

| | |
|---|---|
| Paralegal | Medical Records Technician |
| Radiologic Technologist | Nuclear Medicine Technologist |
| EEG Technologist | Registered Nurse |
| Surgical Technologist | Licensed Practical Nurse |

# Chapter 6

# The top 45 part-time careers

Here they are—the most promising careers for part-timers in the '90s. For more detail on any of 250 occupations, check the *Occupational Outlook Handbook*, published by the Department of Labor, in the business section of your library.

## How to read a listing

**Description.** This brief introduction covers the tasks workers typically perform on the job, including tools and equipment used and the end products or results of their efforts. You'll get a sense for how technological innovations have changed the jobs and you'll learn about any emerging specialties.

Keep in mind, workers in the same occupation may have different responsibilities depending on the employer, the size of the firm and the workers' seniority. In small organizations, for example, workers may perform a wider range of duties.

**Required skills/personal attributes.** From mechanical aptitude to a pleasing personality, most workers need a range of skills and personal attributes to perform well. Overall, you'll find an increasing emphasis on computer literacy as more packaged software programs suited to specific business needs become available.

**Work environment.** What kind of surroundings can you expect on the job? Some people work in noisy environments, or deal with emotional stress. Some must travel extensively. If you're choosing a new career, consider each of these factors very carefully.

If you're considering working from your home, you should be prepared for isolation and other conditions not common in the world of full-time work. See Part 4 for more information on working at home.

**Education/training/certification.** Will you need a degree, a license, continuing education? You'll learn about the types of education and training available, which are preferred by employers and which are required for advancement. If voluntary certification is available, it may be to your benefit to pursue it—especially in highly competitive occupations.

**Salary range.** Some workers are paid a straight annual salary. Others are paid an hourly wage or a commission based on a percentage of what they sell. In most cases, you'll find one salary range based on limited data available for 1990. Use this as a guideline.

Salaries can vary substantially by region or city, level of experience and responsibility—even union influence. So, if compensation is a key element in your career selection, it would be wise to spend time doing some research. Write to the industry association listed at the end of each job description or try talking to professionals at various levels.

Most full-time workers receive benefits, such as health care and vacation time, paid for by their employers. When you negotiate a salary for a part-time work arrangement you may be able to negotiate a higher hourly rate or a salary-benefit package. See Part 3 for tips on negotiating.

**Opportunities for advancement/career growth.** If advancement is likely to be limited or available only with additional education, you need to know about it. You'll learn the typical path for advancement within each occupation, as well as common patterns of movement to other related occupations or self-employment.

This section will also sketch trends that will affect the growth of each occupation throughout the '90s. You can get a sense for how much competition you'll face in getting ahead and how vulnerable your job is likely to be during a recession.

**Drawbacks for part-timers.** Here, you'll get straight talk about potential pitfalls for part-timers, such as irregular client schedules, extensive travel or on-call duty rotations.

**Advantages for part-timers.** Some jobs lend themselves to part-time or temporary employment or self-employment. You'll learn how many other workers are already pursuing part-time careers and whether the occupation is more conducive to seasonal or shift work.

Don't be put off by the fact that a small number of workers in a particular occupation are pursuing part-time work. Use the information in Parts 3 and 4 of this book to negotiate your own part-time arrangement.

**For more information.** This is where to write for more information on a particular career and industry. There are many other resources for information, including industry directories, professional publications and computer databases. Check the index at the back of this book for additional resources.

# ACCOUNTANTS

Two types of accountants prepare, analyze and verify financial reports. **Public accountants** may be self-employed or work for a public accounting firm. **Management accountants** work inside companies.

Some public accountants specialize in preparing income tax returns and advising companies on the tax advantages of business strategies, such as merging with another company or marketing products internationally. Others advise companies on how to design accounting and data processing systems, safeguard assets or obtain financing. Some accountants teach and conduct research at professional schools.

***Required skills/personal attributes.*** Accountants should be able to analyze, compare and interpret facts and figures quickly and accurately. They should be able to work with little supervision. Good interpersonal skills and the ability to clearly communicate results via oral and written presentations to clients and management are essential. Computer literacy is a requirement for a growing number of accountants who use computers to work with data extracted from large mainframe computers.

***Work environment.*** Management and public accountants work in comfortable, well-lighted offices. Public accountants often work in the offices of clients. Accountants who are self-employed may work at home.

***Education/training/certification.*** Most companies require at least a bachelor's degree in accounting. Some prefer a master's degree or MBA.

Certified Public Accountants (CPAs) are licensed and regulated by the State Board of Accountancy in most states. Candidates with the required course work and job experience must complete a rigorous, two-and-a-half-day examination prepared by the American Institute of Certified Public Accountants.

About 38 states license Public Accountants (PAs) and Registered Public Accountants (RPAs) to carry out similar duties requiring less stringent qualifications. Four states allow Accounting Practitioners with less formal training to handle a more limited practice.

Nearly all states require CPAs, PAs and RPAs to complete continuing education to renew their license. Voluntary certification from a professional society can attest to professional competence in a specialized field of accounting.

***Salary range.*** According to a 1991 College Placement Council Salary survey, accountants with bachelor's degrees working full-time start at $26,600. Those with master's degrees start at $31,100. Junior Public Accountants can earn from $31,100 to $45,600. Senior-level accountants and partners in accounting firms can earn more than $100,000.

***Opportunities for advancement/career growth.*** Because a growing number of business owners and corporate managers need to have up-to-date financial information to make strategic decisions in a more challenging marketplace, opportunities for accountants look bright well into the '90s—especially those who specialize in international business, legislation and computer systems.

CPAs will continue to have the widest range of opportunities. Accountants with bachelor's degrees should focus on helping a growing number of new and established small businesses.

***Drawbacks for part-timers.*** Only 10 percent of accountants are self-employed and less than 10 percent work part-time. Tax specialists often work grueling hours during the tax season. Companies may still be reluctant to let in-house accountants telecommute or work part-time. Depending on their duties and clientele, accountants may be required to spend a considerable amount of time traveling.

***Advantages for part-timers.*** Accountants are rarely affected by economic downturns. Those serving a growing number of new businesses may arrange to work on a project-by-project basis. Most full-time accountants are concentrated in the urban headquarters of public accounting firms and corporations, leaving suburban areas ripe for home-based entrepreneurs serving small local businesses.

***For more information.*** Write to the American Institute of Certified Public Accountants, 1211 Avenue of the Americas, New York, NY 10036-8775.

# ACTORS/DANCERS

Actors may use a range of facial and vocal expressions, song, dance and other types of body movements—as well as costumes, props and makeup—to bring a character to life for audiences in a play or other form of dramatic entertainment.

Performing as a group or solo, dancers express ideas, stories, rhythm and sound with their bodies in the style of classical ballet, modern dance, dance adaptations for musical shows, folk, ethnic or jazz dance.

***Required skills/personal attributes.*** All performers need stage presence. They must have a good memory and be willing to follow direction. Both actors and dancers need physical stamina, patience, creativity and total commitment to their craft.

Dancers must demonstrate flexibility, grace, agility, coordination, a sense of rhythm and the creative ability to express themselves through movement.

***Work environment.*** Both actors and dancers work long, often irregular hours under hot stage or studio lights. Extended travel is necessary when plays go on the road. They must find ways to live with the anxiety of intermittent employment and frequent rejection when auditioning for work.

Actors may work in adverse weather conditions. Dancers have one and a half hours of lessons every day and spend many additional hours practicing and rehearsing. The work is often strenuous.

***Education/training/certification.*** Formal training and experience are generally necessary for actors. Dramatic arts schools in New York and Los Angeles and colleges and universities throughout the country offer bachelor's and higher degrees in dramatic and theater arts. Local and regional theater experience is a plus.

Most dancers start their careers at a very young age. Because of a time-consuming training schedule, a dancer's formal academic education may be minimal. Many colleges and universities offer bachelor's and higher degrees in dance. But ballet dancers who postpone their first audition until graduation may find themselves at a disadvantage.

*Salary range.* Minimum salaries, work hours and employment conditions for actors are covered in collective bargaining agreements between producers and one of the following actors' unions: The Actors' Equity Association, for stage actors; the Screen Actors Guild for actors in motion pictures, television and commercials, and the American Federation of Television and Radio Artists (AFTRA). Actors are free to negotiate a salary higher than the minimum.

In 1991, the minimum weekly salary for actors in Broadway productions was $850; in small off-Broadway plays, from $310 to $546. In 1992, motion picture and television actors earned a minimum daily rate of $448, or $1,558 for a five-day week. They receive additional compensation for reruns.

Earnings for dancers are governed by one of the following unions: The American Guild of Musical Artists, Inc., AFL-CIO, for dancers in ballet, classical ballet and modern dance; the American Federation of Television and Radio Artists, Screen Actors or Screen Extras Guild for television and motion picture performers; and the Actors' Equity Association for dancers working in musical comedy stage productions.

In the 1992, the minimum weekly salary for a dancer was $555. First-year dancers earned an average $230 per single performance and $60 per rehearsal hour. The minimum weekly salary for TV performers was $569 for a one-hour show.

*Opportunities for advancement/career growth.* Only a few performers achieve recognition as stars. Most actors pick up whatever parts they can, striving to work on larger productions in more prestigious theaters. Some actors move into related jobs, such as drama coach or director.

In the '90s, an increasing demand for American productions from abroad, a growing domestic market for dramatic productions fueled by the growth of cable television, home movie rentals and syndication as well as a renewed interest in the theatre should combine to significantly stimulate the demand for actors.

*Drawbacks for part-timers.* Actors and dancers face keen competition. Only the most talented will find regular employment.

Rehearsals require long hours and usually take place daily, including weekends and holidays. For shows on the road, weekend travel is often required. Most performances take place in the evening, so dancers must become accustomed to working late hours.

Because employment is often irregular, overall earnings are low. Actors and dancers often must supplement their incomes by taking additional jobs unrelated to dance. Most dancers stop performing in their late 30s.

***Advantages for part-timers.*** The acting lifestyle offers a number of opportunities for part-time workers who are open to flexible hours and seasonal employment. Once a show opens, actors usually work 24 hours a week, most of them in the evening.

Summer stock theater companies are busy in suburban and resort areas. Many cities have nonprofit professional theater companies. Motion picture studios are located in Florida and Texas and other parts of the country.

A dancer works about 30 hours a week, including rehearsals, matinee and evening performances. Dancers with professional experience can find part-time opportunities as a choreographer, dance teacher, coach or artistic director.

***For more information.*** Write to the Associated Actors and Artists of America, 165 W. 46th St., New York, NY 10036, or, the American Dance Guild, 33 W. 21st St., Third Floor, New York, NY 10010.

# ADULT EDUCATION TEACHERS

Working in vocational-technical schools, basic or continuing education programs, these educators teach adults new skills. Some teachers prepare people to fill jobs that don't require a college degree. Some help drop-outs prepare for the General Educational Development (GED) Examination, the equivalent of a high school diploma. Some teach new Americans English. And a growing number introduce a wide range of adults to new hobbies, such as cooking, dancing, exercise and photography.

51

***Required skills/personal attributes.*** Adult education teachers should be able to communicate easily with a variety of students and be able to motivate them to learn. They must be patient, understanding and supportive, especially with students who are completing basic education. Organizational and administrative skills are a plus.

***Work environment.*** In the classroom, adult education teachers work with students who are motivated to learn, as well as students who require more attention because they lack proper study habits and self-confidence.

***Education/training/certification.*** Requirements may vary by state and subject. In general, adult education instructors need to have work or other experience in their field, and a professional license or certificate in fields in which it is appropriate.

Most states require adult basic education teachers to have a bachelor's degree from an approved teacher training program and require teacher certification. Adult education teachers should update their skills through continuing education seminars, conferences and graduate courses in adult education, training and development.

***Salary range.*** In 1990, full-time, salaried adult education teachers earned from $12,300 to $45,600 a year. Earnings vary widely according to academic credentials and experience, the subject taught and even region. Part-time teachers are paid hourly or receive a day rate and sometimes expenses.

***Opportunities for advancement/career growth.*** As an increasing number of adults register for courses leading to career advancement and personal enrichment, adult education teachers will enjoy a wealth of teaching opportunities.

Changes in the immigration policy that require basic competency in English and civics, as well as a tough job market, will spur growth in basic education programs.

The most promising opportunities for adult education teachers will be in computer technology, automotive mechanics and medical technology.

***Drawbacks for part-timers.*** Adult education teachers do not receive benefits and typically are not paid for the time they spend preparing for class.

***Advantages for part-timers.*** Almost half of all adult education teachers work part-time and many work only intermittently. Some hold other jobs related to the subject they teach. Many are self-employed.

Class schedules are flexible—ranging from two- to four-hour one-time workshops to semester-long courses for credit. Many classes meet at night or on weekends.

***For more information.*** Write to the American Association of Adult and Continuing Education, 1112 16th St. NW, Suite 420, Washington, DC  20036. Information on adult basic education programs and certification requirements is available from the state departments of education and local school districts.

# AUTOMOTIVE MECHANICS

Automotive mechanics repair and service cars and occasionally light trucks, such as vans and pickups. During routine service, mechanics inspect, lubricate and adjust engines and other components. They may also repair and replace parts, such as belts and hoses, before they cause breakdowns. In the process of repairing a vehicle, the mechanic may use a variety of hand and power tools, machine tools, welding and flame-cutting equipment, jacks and hoists and electronic service equipment.

***Required skills/personal attributes.*** In addition to a thorough knowledge of how automobiles work, mechanics must have good reading and basic math skills and be familiar with the latest techniques and technology, such as electronics. Mechanical aptitude combined with the ability to diagnose hard-to-find troubles is also essential.

***Work environment.*** While most auto mechanics work indoors in well-ventilated and lighted shops, they frequently work with dirty, greasy parts. Often they must work in awkward positions and lift heavy parts and tools. Minor cuts, burns and bruises are common. Serious accidents are avoided by observing safety practices.

*Education/training/certification.* Formal training programs offered in high schools, community colleges and public and private vocational-technical schools are recommended for beginning mechanics. By combining classroom instruction with hands-on practice, some trade and technical school programs concentrate the instruction into six months.

Various automotive manufacturers and their participating dealers sponsor two-year associate degree programs. Employers frequently send experienced automotive mechanics to factory training centers to learn the latest techniques for repairing new models.

Voluntary certification by the Automotive Service Association is widely recognized as a standard of achievement in eight different service areas. Certification may be updated by taking the exam every five years.

*Salary range.* In 1990, full-time mechanics employed by dealers in large metropolitan areas earned from $13.27 to $18.62 an hour, depending on their skills. Many receive a commission.

*Opportunities for advancement/career growth.* As more young drivers take to the road in newer vehicles, there will be steady opportunities for mechanics who are skilled in the latest automotive technology. In addition, the average age of automobiles in operation continues to be high, requiring more service and repair.

Beginners start as trainee mechanics, helpers or gasoline service attendants. In two years they may advance to journeyman service mechanics. However, graduates of accredited post-secondary mechanic training programs are often able to earn a promotion to journeyman after only a few months.

In large shops, mechanics generally specialize in areas such as transmissions, tune-ups or brake repair. Mastering difficult specialties requires about two years of work experience. Master automotive mechanics are certified in all eight specialty areas.

Experienced mechanics with leadership ability may advance to shop supervisor or service manager. Those who work well with customers may become repair service estimators or open their own repair shops.

**Drawbacks for part-timers.** Most mechanics work full-time. The 20 percent of self-employed mechanics may work long hours to accommodate the schedules of individual customers.

**Advantages for part-timers:** Economic conditions have little effect on opportunities for mechanics. Self-employed mechanics with a regular clientele may be able to operate on flexible schedules by offering routine maintenance.

**For more information.** Write to the Automotive Service Association, Inc., P.O. Box 929, Bedford, TX 76021.

# CARPENTERS

Carpenters cut, fit and assemble wood and other materials used in the construction of buildings, highways, bridges and other structures. Working for a special trade or a general building contractor, carpenters typically follow blueprints or instructions to measure, mark and arrange materials. They must know local building codes that dictate where certain materials can be used.

Using hand and power tools, carpenters cut and shape wood, plastic, ceiling tile, fiberglass or drywall and then join materials using hardware and adhesives. After checking for accuracy, they make any necessary adjustments.

**Required skills/personal attributes.** Carpenters must have excellent eye-hand coordination and manual dexterity. They must be in good physical condition, with a good sense of balance.

**Work environment.** Prolonged standing, climbing and bending makes this a strenuous occupation. Carpenters risk injury from falls, as well as from working with sharp materials and power tools. They work outdoors in all kinds of weather. Pre-fabricated components and better tools reduce fatigue and make workers more efficient.

**Education/training/certification.** Some carpenters pick up skills by working with those more experienced. Most employers recommend an apprenticeship that combines classroom and on-the-job training for up to four years. Applicants for apprenticeships must be at least 17 and meet local requirements. These programs are limited. For information, contact the nearest office of the state em-ployment service or state apprenticeship agency.

***Salary range.*** In 1990, full-time carpenters earned from $238 to $739 a week.

***Opportunities for advancement/career growth.*** Because they are exposed to the entire building process, carpenters may move on to become supervisors or general construction supervisors. Some become independent contractors.

Although the construction of housing and commercial and industrial buildings is dependent on mortgage funds, interest rates and government spending, carpenters should find steady opportunities for work throughout the '90s because of population growth.

***Drawbacks for part-timers.*** Carpenters experience unexpected periods of unemployment due to economic conditions and bad weather. Opportunities for employment often vary by geographic area.

***Advantages for part-timers.*** About one in three carpenters is self-employed. Some change employers with each job. Carpenters are employed everywhere—in large and small communities.

***For more information:*** Write to the Associated Builders and Contractors, Inc., 729 15th St. NW, Washington, DC 20005.

# COMPUTER PROGRAMMERS

Computer programmers write, update and maintain detailed instructions (called programs or software) that computers use to perform a variety of tasks. **Applications programmers** specialize in writing software programs for business, engineering and science organizations.

Most programming involves updating and modifying code for existing programs. Using a programming language, such as COBOL, programmers write code for step-by-step instructions the computer needs to process and deliver data in the desired format. Programmers must "debug" programs by running tests using sample data and fixing incorrect parts of the programs. They also prepare an instruction sheet for the operator who will run the program and may assist in writing a user's manual.

In smaller organizations, programmer-analysts may handle both tasks. **Systems programmers** maintain the software that controls the operation of the entire computer.

***Required skills/personal attributes:*** Computer programmers must be adept at thinking logically, and capable of working with abstract concepts. Patience, persistence and ability to maintain accuracy even under pressure, are essential. Ingenuity is important as are, increasingly, interpersonal skills.

***Work environment.*** Programmers generally work in comfortable offices.

***Education/training/certification.*** Public and private vocational schools, community and junior colleges and universities all offer training for computer programmers. A bachelor's degree is commonly required, along with knowledge and experience in a related business area.

A Certificate in Computer Programming is an indication of experience and professional competence for senior-level programmers. It is awarded by the Institute for Certification of Computer Professionals. College graduates with little or no experience may be tested for certification as an Associate Computer Professional.

Because technology is changing so rapidly, all professionals must continuously update knowledge by taking courses sponsored by employers or software vendors.

***Salary range.*** Systems programmers and programmers working in the West and Northeast earn more than the average applications programmer or programmers working for the government. Salaries range from $17,000 to $52,100.

***Opportunities for advancement/career growth.*** Ever-increasing demand for information, further automation, and advances in scientific research will drive growth. Prospects look bright throughout the '90s for skilled programmers. College graduates should be familiar with a variety of programming languages, particularly newer languages that apply to computer networking, database management and artificial intelligence.

In large organizations, programmers can advance to the position of lead programmer with supervisory responsibilities. With business experience, they may be promoted to the managerial level. With specialized knowledge and experience, some programmers opt to go into research and development.

***Drawbacks for part-timers.*** Programmers who are testing new programs and modifications often need to adjust their schedules—working early or late to gain access to the central computer during off-hours. They may occasionally work long hours in order to meet deadlines.

***Advantages for part-timers.*** Those who work full-time often work flexible hours. A small, but growing number are employed on a temporary project basis (from a few months for over a year) through a consulting firm or as self-employed contractors.

***For more information.*** Write to the Institute for the Certification of Computer Professionals, 2200 East Devon Ave., Suite 268, Des Plaines, IL 60018.

# CONSTRUCTION CONTRACTORS

Whether self-employed, salaried employees of a construction contracting firm, or working under contract for an owner, developer, contractor or management firm, construction contractors are involved in every aspect of a project. They plan, budget, schedule and coordinate.

Depending on the project, they may monitor the delivery of materials and equipment, obtain all necessary permits and licenses and hire and supervise others working on the job.

***Required skills/personal attributes.*** In addition to understanding engineering and architectural drawings and specifications, construction contractors must able to quickly analyze and resolve specific problems and find ways to make work proceed faster and more efficiently. Contractors need good interpersonal skills in order to confer with design professionals, cost estimators and employers. They must be decisive, adaptable and able to work effectively in a fast-paced environment. Organization, good writing skills and basic computer literacy are also important.

***Work environment.*** Construction contractors monitor the overall progress of a project from a main office or in a spartan on-site field office. They may have to travel from site to site. Because there is always danger inherent in working with tools and machinery, a constructor is often on-call to deal with accidents or delays.

***Education/training/certification.*** Entrants are encouraged to have a bachelor's degree in construction science, with an emphasis on construction management. Experience as a craft worker, such as a carpenter or mason, and proven supervisory ability are also important. Many contractors attend training and educational programs sponsored by trade associations.

***Salary range.*** The size and nature of a project, geographical location and economic conditions all determine annual earnings that can range from $35,000 to $100,000 for experienced contractors.

***Opportunities for advancement/career growth.*** A projected increase in spending on the nation's infrastructure (highways, schools, airports), will spur the demand for more construction contractors in the years ahead. Contractors will also find work building residential housing and commercial buildings and maintaining and repairing existing structures.

Those who have expertise working with new materials and technology, such as electronically operated "smart" buildings, will have the best opportunities.

***Drawbacks for part-timers.*** Project deadlines can call for very intense, full-time work schedules. Contractors often face unexpected periods of unemployment because of economic conditions and bad weather. Employment opportunities may vary by geographic area.

***Advantages for part-timers.*** The short-term nature of many construction projects, especially residential and maintenance projects, as well as seasonal fluctuations in construction activity, may be an advantage for self-employed contractors. Some contractors may be able to arrange to work longer hours for fewer days per week.

***For more information.*** Write to the American Institute of Constructors, 9887 North Gandy Blvd., Suite 104, St. Petersburg, FL 33702, or The Associated General Contractors of America, 1957 E St. NW, Washington, DC 20006.

# COSMETOLOGISTS

Most cosmetologists shampoo, cut and style men's and women's hair. Many offer additional personal services, such as straightening, permanent waving and hair coloring. They keep records of treatments for on-going service.

Some full-service salons employ cosmetologists who are trained to provide manicures and pedicures, scalp and facial treatments, makeup analysis and application and electrolysis. Depending on the size of the salon, cosmetologists may also set appointments and sell hair products and other cosmetic supplies. Those who operate their own salons have managerial duties that include hiring, supervising and ordering supplies.

***Required skills/personal attributes.*** Cosmetologists should enjoy dealing with people and be willing to follow instructions. A sense of form and artistry, as well as finger dexterity are essential. Good health, physical stamina and business skills are also important.

**Work environment.** Salons are generally clean and pleasant with good lighting and ventilation. Most cosmetologists stand a great deal of the day and some are exposed to harsh chemicals for prolonged periods.

**Education/training/certification.** Day and evening programs in vocational schools usually last six months to one year and include classroom study, demonstrations and practical work on men's and women's hair. Cosmetologist must stay up-to-date on the latest fashion and beauty techniques.

All states require cosmetologists to be licensed. Although qualifications vary by state, most award a license to high school graduates who have completed a state-licensed cosmetology program, passed a physical examination and written test and demonstrated their ability to perform basic cosmetology services.

Some states require manicurists and cosmetologists who provide facial care to take a separate test for licensing. In rare cases, apprenticeship can be a substitute for formal training.

Some states have reciprocity agreements that allow cosmetologists who are licensed in one state to practice in another.

**Salary range.** Cosmetologists typically receive income from commission (50 to 70 percent of the money they take in) or wages (from $7 to $14 an hour in 1990) and tips. Earnings depend on the size and location of the shop, the reputation of the cosmetologist, the number of hours worked and the tipping habits of patrons.

**Opportunities for advancement/career growth.** Most cosmetologists work in beauty salons and department stores. A few work in hospitals, hotels and prisons. With a steady clientele, a cosmetologist can eventually open his or her own salon.

Population growth, more women in the work force and rising incomes will continue to make prospects bright for cosmetologists throughout the '90s. Opportunities should be plentiful for those who specialize in nail and skin care.

**Drawbacks for part-timers.** Stylists who set fashion trends usually work in New York, Los Angeles and other centers of fashion and the performing arts. Demand for full-service care may be limited in rural areas.

***Advantages for part-timers.*** About half of all cosmetologists are self-employed. One in three work part-time. Cosmetologists who schedule their own appointments may work only a few days a week, a few hours a day or take advantage of busy evening and weekend trade. Some find additional part-time opportunities teaching, as sales representatives for cosmetic firms or as beauty consultants.

***For more information.*** Write to the National Cosmetology Association, Inc., 3510 Olive St., St. Louis, MO 63103.

# DENTAL ASSISTANTS

Dental assistants perform a variety of clinical, office and laboratory duties. Working at a dentist's side, they prepare patients for treatment, obtain dental records and hand the dentist the proper instruments and materials. They may also sterilize and disinfect instruments and equipment, prepare tray setups for procedures, provide post-operative instruction and process dental x-rays. In most states, dental assistants can remove sutures, apply anesthetic and remove excess cement used in the filling process.

In the laboratory, dental assistants make casts of patients' teeth from impressions taken by the dentist, clean and polish removable appliances and make temporary crowns. They also may perform office duties, such as setting and confirming appointments and ordering supplies.

***Required skills/personal attributes.*** As a dentist's "third hand," a dental assistant must be organized, reliable and have good manual dexterity. It's also important to be able to put patients at ease and work well with co-workers.

***Work environment.*** Dental assistants work in well-lighted, clean offices and laboratories. They may spend a great of time standing. Gloves, masks and the proper use of lead shields and safety procedures should minimize the dangers from infectious diseases and radiographic equipment.

***Education/training/certification.*** Dental assistants may learn their skills on the job or in dental assisting programs offered by community or junior colleges, technical institutes or the military.

The American Dental Association's Commission on Dental Accreditation endorses programs that include classroom, laboratory and pre-clinical instruction. Students gain practical experience in dental schools, clinics and dental offices and earn a certificate or diploma in about a year. Two-year programs lead to an associate degree. Some private vocational schools offer non-accredited, four- to six-month courses in dental assisting.

Although not typically required for employment, voluntary certification is available through the Dental Assisting National Board. Candidates for certification must graduate from an accredited program or have two years of full-time experience and have completed a course in cardiopulmonary resuscitation (CPR).

***Salary range.*** In 1990, full-time dental assistants earned about $300 a week. In 1989, the average hourly rate was $8.90.

***Opportunities for advancement/career growth.*** Higher incomes, more dental insurance and a growing population of middle-aged and elderly patients promise a bright future for dental assistants. Dental assistants who wish to advance to dental hygienists need further education.

***Drawbacks for part-timers.*** None.

***Advantages for part-timers.*** About one in three dental assistants work part-time, sometimes in more than one dentist's office. Many work on weekends and in the evening.

***For more information.*** Write to the American Dental Assistants Association, 919 N. Michigan Ave., Chicago, IL 60611.

# DENTAL HYGIENISTS

Dental hygienists provide preventive dental care and teach patients how to practice good oral hygiene. After examining a patient's teeth and mouth, hygienists record the presence of disease or abnormalities and remove calculus, stain and plaque from above and below the gumline. They may develop dental x-rays, place temporary fillings and periodontal dressings, remove sutures and polish and recontour amalgam restorations. In some states, dental hygienists administer local anesthetics and nitrous oxide/oxygen analgesia, and place and carve filling materials.

Dental hygienists use a variety of hand and rotary instruments to clean teeth, as well as syringes to administer local anesthetic and x-ray machines. They also use models of teeth and dental floss to instruct patients in proper oral hygiene.

***Required skills/personal attributes.*** Dental hygienists should have good interpersonal skills, particularly when dealing with patients who are under stress. Good health, personal grooming and manual dexterity are essential.

***Work environment.*** Dental hygienists work in clean, well-lighted offices. They wear safety glasses, surgical masks and gloves as protection from infectious diseases. They also are trained in proper radiological procedures, recommended aseptic techniques and the use of appropriate protective devices when administering nitrous oxide/oxygen analgesia.

***Education/training/certification.*** Dental hygienists must be licensed by the state in which they practice. Candidates must graduate from an accredited dental hygiene school and pass both a written examination administered by the American Dental Association Joint Commission on National Dental Examinations and a clinical examination administered by a state or regional testing agency. Most programs grant an associate degree and require candidates to have up to two years of college to enter the program.

***Salary range.*** Dental hygienists may be paid hourly, daily, by salary or commission. Earnings depend on geographical locations, employment setting, education and experience. In 1989, the average hourly salary was $17.50.

***Opportunities for advancement/career growth.*** Higher incomes, more dental insurance and a growing population of middle-aged and elderly patients promise a bright future for dental hygienists who can handle routine tasks that free dentists for surgery and other profitable procedures. With a bachelor's degree or master's degree in dental hygiene, hygienists can pursue research and teaching.

***Drawbacks for part-timers.*** None.

***Advantages for part-timers.*** Flexible scheduling is a distinctive feature of this job. Part-time, evening and weekend work are widely available. About a third of all hygienists work less then 35 hours a week.

Dentists frequently hire dental hygienists to work two or three days a week. Some hygienists work for more than one dentist. Others work in public health agencies, school systems, hospitals and clinics.

***For more information.*** Write to the Division of Professional Development, American Dental Hygienists' Association, 444 N. Michigan Ave., Suite 3400, Chicago, IL 60611.

# DESIGNERS

A wide range of designers bring a visually pleasing appearance and serviceability to a variety of products and materials—from clothing to flowers to product packaging.

For example, **industrial designers** create products and packaging that are functional and appealing. **Interior designers** plan space and renovate and furnish interiors of homes and commercial establishments. **Fashion designers** work with individual clients or establish a "line" of clothing for a season. **Floral designers** cut and arrange fresh, dried and artificial flowers. **Graphic designers** create two-dimensional designs that attract attention and communicate ideas.

Sketches, scale models or detailed plans for several designs are presented to an art or design director, product development team or client for final selection. Many designers use sophisticated drawing programs, computer-aided design (CAD) or computer-aided industrial design (CAID).

Designers often supervise production artists or craft workers who carry out their designs. Self-employed designers may devote considerable time to developing contacts and handling administrative tasks.

***Required skills/personal attributes.*** Creativity, imagination, problem-solving skills and the ability to communicate ideas visually and verbally are hallmarks of all good designers.

Designers should be skilled in the elements of good design, such as color, balance and proportion, and up-to-date on trends in design. Sketching ability is helpful. They should be able to meet deadlines. Business sense and sales ability are important for those who run their own businesses.

***Work environment.*** Designers work in manufacturing and design firms that generally provide well-lighted, comfortable settings. Some transact business in a client's home or office, in their own office or other locations, such as showrooms.

***Education/training/certification.*** Industrial designers generally need a bachelor's degree in fine arts and must be knowledgeable about federal, state and local codes as well as toxicity and flammability standards for furniture and furnishings.

Fashion designers may earn a two- or four-year degree and must be knowledgeable about textiles, fabrics and ornamentation, as well as trends in fashion.

Interior designers must be licensed in the District of Columbia and are regulated in 14 states. Candidates need up to four years of post-secondary education, at least two years of practical experience and completion of the National Council for Interior Design Qualification Examination.

Graphic designers learn skills in post-secondary art school programs or by earning a bachelor's in fine art, graphic design or visual communication.

Some colleges and universities offer degrees in floriculture and provide training in flower marketing and shop management. Floral design is taught at private trade and technical schools.

***Salary range.*** Experienced designers in all specialties can expect to earn $16,700 to $50,000 per year. Floral designers earn less.

Designers who move into managerial and executive positions or are self-employed can expect to earn an average $86,000 or more.

***Opportunities for advancement/career growth.*** Beginning designers usually receive up to three years of training on the job before advancing to higher-level positions. Designers in large firms can advance to art director, department head or open their own business. Opportunities for employment are expected to grow faster than the average for all design occupations. Opportunities for advancement may be limited for floral designers because of low pay.

***Drawbacks for part-timers.*** Designers can expect to face competition throughout their careers. All confront rejection and frustration when their creativity is limited by a client or employer. Opportunities may be limited for graphic designers who work with companies that employ in-house desktop publishing experts.

Floral designers often work holidays and weekends. Fashion designers may have to travel extensively to visit manufacturing facilities abroad. Independent consultants are paid by the project and are under constant pressure to retain and find new clients.

***Advantages for part-timers.*** Nearly a third of all designers are self-employed. Many begin by doing freelance work part-time while still working a full-time job. Designers must adjust their schedules for their clients, but they are free to schedule other hours for maximum productivity, working evenings or weekends, if necessary.

***For more information:*** Write to the National Association of Schools of Art and Design, 11250 Roger Bacon Dr., Suite 21, Reston, VA 22090, or The American Institute of Graphic Arts, 1059 Third Ave., New York, NY 10021.

# EEG TECHNOLOGISTS

EEG technologists operate the electroencephalograph (EEG) machines that record electrical impulses transmitted by the brain. Physicians use EEG readings and related tests to diagnose brain tumors, strokes and epilepsy and to measure the effects of infectious diseases and impairments such as Alzheimer's disease.

After taking a patient's medical history, the EEG technologist applies electrodes to various spots on the patient's head and selects the appropriate combination of instrument controls to produce the necessary record. It is often necessary to correct for electrical or mechanical events that come from eye movement and elsewhere.

To assure correct EEG readings in the operating room, technologists must be knowledgeable about how anesthesia can affect brain waves. The EEG technologist may attach electrodes to other parts of a patient's body to record activity from central and peripheral nervous systems, while patients carry out normal activities over a 24-hour period. Specialized technologists also administer sleep studies to monitor respiration, heart and brain wave activity in various stages of sleep.

***Required skills/personal attributes.*** An EEG technologist needs manual dexterity and good vision. Good writing skills, the ability to work well with patients and other health professionals and an aptitude for working with electronic equipment are essential.

***Work environment.*** EEG technologists usually work in clean, well-lighted surroundings. They may spend half their working hours on their feet. Bending and lifting are necessary when working with patients who are very ill. In hospitals, EEG technologists may take the equipment to a patient's bedside.

***Education/training/certification.*** While an EEG technologist may learn skills on the job, some complete formal training programs. Applicants for trainee positions in hospitals need a high school diploma. Formal post-secondary training is offered in hospitals and community colleges. Programs usually include one to two years of classroom experience and award an associate degree or certificate.

The American Board of Registration of Electroencephalographic Technologists awards the Registered EEG Technologist and accredits the subspecialty Registered Evoked Potential Technologist. Certification is usually required for teaching or supervisory positions.

***Salary range.*** In 1991, full-time EEG technologists working in private hospitals earned approximately $10.75 an hour. Part-time technologists earned about $11.35 an hour. Laboratory supervisors and training program directors generally earn higher salaries.

***Opportunities for advancement/career growth.*** Most EEG technologists work in the EEG or neurology laboratories of hospitals. In larger hospitals, they may advance, by performing more difficult tests, to chief EEG technologist.

EEG technologists also work in the offices and clinics of neurologists and neurosurgeons, health maintenance organizations and psychiatric facilities. Some transfer to other jobs, such as LPN (licensed practical nurse), decide to teach or conduct research.

A steady increase in the number of neurodiagnostic tests that are typically performed on an aging population will be reflected in the rapid growth in employment opportunities for formally trained EEG technologists.

***Drawbacks for part-timers.*** Many EEG technologists working in hospitals are on-call evenings, weekends and holidays.

***Advantages for part-timers.*** Predicted growth in employment opportunities in the offices and clinics of neurologists, where much of the testing is scheduled, may make it easier for EEG technologists to negotiate part-time schedules.

***For more information.*** Write to the Executive Office, American Society of Electroneurodiagnostic Technologists, Inc., Sixth at Quint, Carroll, IA 51401.

# EMPLOYMENT INTERVIEWERS

Personnel consultants, employment brokers and headhunters are other titles for these professionals, who help job-seekers find employment and help employers find qualified staff. Working in private personnel firms, employment interviewers attempt to match one or more qualified applicants on file with the firm to a specific job listing provided by a prospective employer.

Employee interviewers work with resumes and other job-related information received from job-seekers, such as interviews, test scores, references and credentials. Some firms specialize in placing particular kinds of professionals—such as secretaries or engineers.

Some employment interviewers work in temporary help firms. Using job orders from client firms, they match the job requirements against the skills of a list of available workers. Temporary help firms test and regularly evaluate workers to determine their job skills, strengths and weaknesses.

***Required skills/personal attributes.*** Employment interviewers should be good salespeople, and be able to communicate well with employers and job-seekers. A pleasant telephone voice and a genuine desire to help people are essential. Office skills and computer literacy are important.

***Work environment.*** Employment interviewers usually work in comfortable, well-lighted offices. Some spend a lot of time out of the office interviewing clients. The industry is competitive and the pace is often hectic, especially in temporary help firms that must fill employers' immediate help on a daily and weekly basis.

***Education/training/certification.*** Firms specializing in placing highly trained individuals, such as lawyers, prefer to hire interviewers who have training or experience in that particular field.

***Salary range.*** The basis for compensation varies. Some interviewers are paid straight commission, usually about 30 percent of what the personnel firm bills the employer. Employment interviewers working in specialized firms may receive salary and commission, because highly skilled positions often take longer to fill. Employee interviewers in temporary help firms earn a straight salary—from $17,000 to $25,000 in 1991.

***Opportunities for advancement/career growth.*** In most firms, advancement is based on regular promotions. Some successful interviewers start their own businesses. Three out of five work for employment firms or temporary help firms.

Employment opportunities are expected to be steady throughout the '90s. Most new jobs will become available in temporary help firms, to handle an increased demand for such workers.

***Drawbacks for part-timers.*** Although companies will continue to depend on personnel firms to find and screen new employees, growth is tied to the health of the economy. In slow times, fewer jobs are available. In times of high unemployment, a glut of qualified applicants may prompt employers to handle hiring in-house.

***Advantages for part-timers.*** Part-timers may arrange to work mornings—the busiest part of the day in temporary help firms. Employment interviewers working with databases may be able to telecommute or arrange flexible hours based on scheduled interviews with employers and job seekers. Headhunters often run their own home-based businesses.

***For more information.*** Write to the National Association of Personnel Consultants, 3133 Mt. Vernon Ave., Alexandria, VA 22305.

# FINE ARTISTS

Fine artists use a wide variety of materials—such as paints, markers, plaster, clay and computers—to create art objects or images of objects, people, nature and events. Although some work may be done at the request of a client, fine artists often create simply to satisfy their own need of self-expression. Fine artists usually specialize in one or two art forms.

***Required skills/personal attributes.*** Creativity, imagination, problem-solving skills and the ability to communicate ideas visually and verbally are hallmarks of all good artists.

Fine artists should be skilled at finding and working with a wide variety of materials, and knowledgeable about composition, color mixing, balance and proportion. Business sense and sales ability are important for those who wish to sell their work to galleries or clients.

***Work environment.*** Fine artists generally work independently in studios, office buildings or at home. Studios are usually well-lighted and ventilated, although odors from paint, ink and other materials may be present.

*Education/training/certification.* It is very difficult to acquire the skill to make a living from fine art without some basic training. Bachelor's and graduate degree programs in fine art are offered by many colleges and universities. Fine artists must also demonstrate their ability by assembling a portfolio of work.

*Salary range.* Earnings for self-employed fine artists vary widely. Those struggling to gain experience and a reputation may be forced to charge amounts less than minimum wage for their work. Many freelancers earn very little as they acquire experience and establish a good reputation. Well-established artists often earn much more than salaried artists.

*Opportunities for advancement/career growth.* Fine artists sell their work in stores, commercial art galleries and museums or directly to collectors. Commercial artists sell on consignment. Fine artists and illustrators advance as their work circulates and they establish a reputation.

Freelance artists must develop a clientele to work regularly on a contract or project basis. Some earn high incomes and can pick and choose their work.

Employment of fine artists is expected to rise, reflecting population growth, rising incomes and growth of appreciation for art. Talented artists should continue to be in great demand.

*Drawbacks for part-timers.* Only the most successful artists are able to support themselves through the sale of their works. Most hold other jobs.

*Advantages for part-timers.* Fine artists may find part-time opportunities teaching art to adults or in elementary or secondary schools. Those with a master's degree or higher may teach at the college or university level. Others may work as art critics, consultants or gallery directors.

*For more information.* Write to the American Institute of Graphic Arts, 1059 Third Ave., New York, NY 10021.

# FLIGHT ATTENDANTS

Flight attendants ensure the safety and comfort of passengers aboard private and commercial airplanes. They are briefed on expected weather conditions and special passenger problems an hour before each flight. Flight attendants make sure that the passenger cabin is in order and that supplies of food and beverages, blankets and reading material are adequate. They also check first-aid kits and other emergency equipment.

As passengers board the aircraft, flight attendants check boarding passes and assist passengers in storing coats and carry-on luggage. Before take-off, flight attendants instruct passengers on the use of emergency equipment and check to see that all passengers have their seat belts fastened.

In the air, they are available to answer questions, care for small children and elderly passengers and serve drinks and meals. In the event of an emergency, they open emergency exits and inflate evacuation chutes.

***Required skills/personal attributes.*** Flight attendants should be friendly, poised, resourceful and be able to deal comfortably with strangers. Excellent health, good vision and a clear speaking voice are important. Increasingly, the ability to speak two or more languages is a plus.

***Work environment.*** Flight attendants divide their time between the ground and the air. They may spend considerable time waiting for planes that arrive late. The work is often strenuous and tiring. Flight attendants must stand and walk during much of a flight, yet remain pleasant and efficient in serving demanding passengers. They are susceptible to injury working aboard a moving aircraft.

***Education/training/certification.*** Although a high school diploma is acccptable, most airlines prefer several years of college or service experience. Most large airlines require newly hired flight attendants to complete a four- to six-week, expense-paid training program. Flight attendants must receive up to 14 hours of training in emergency procedures and passenger relations annually.

***Salary range.*** In 1990, beginning flight attendants earned an average $13,000 a year. Some senior attendants earn as much as $35,000 a year. Flight attendants receive additional compensation for overtime and night and international flights. They and their immediate families are entitled to reduced air fares.

***Opportunities for advancement/career growth.*** The majority of flight attendants are employed by commercial airlines and must be stationed in the airline's home-base city. A small number work for large companies that operate their own aircraft for business purposes. Some become flight service instructors, customer service directors or recruiting representatives.

Employment opportunities for flight attendants are expected to be bright throughout the '90s, because of an unexpected growth in business and pleasure travel. Competition for these "glamour" jobs will remain keen. Those with at least two years of college have the best chance.

***Drawbacks for part-timers.*** Flight attendants may work nights, weekends and holidays. Though they only fly 75 to 85 hours a month, they may spend another 75 to 85 hours a month on the ground, preparing planes for flight and waiting for late planes to arrive. Flight attendants may be away from home one-third of time. During recessions, flight attendants may be laid off until demand increases.

Reserve attendants must be available on short notice. It may take up to five years to advance out of reserve status. Usually only the most experienced attendants get their choice of base locations and flights.

***Advantages for part-timers.*** Because of variations in scheduling and limitations on flying time, many attendants have 11 or more days off a month.

***For more information:*** Write to the Future Aviation Professionals of America, 4959 Massachusetts Blvd., Atlanta, GA 30337.

# GARDENERS AND GROUNDSKEEPERS

Gardeners who work on large construction projects, such as office buildings and shopping malls, follow plans drawn up by landscape architects. They plant trees, hedges and flowering plants. For residential customers, they may terrace hillsides, build retaining walls and install patios and landscaping.

Gardeners working for homeowners, estates and public gardens feed, water and prune flowering plants and trees and mow and water lawns. Lawn service workers specialize in providing full-service maintenance of lawns and shrubs for a fee.

Groundskeepers may perform a variety of duties working on athletic fields, golf courses, cemeteries and parks, including maintaining lawn grooming equipment and tools.

Both gardeners and groundskeepers use hand tools such as shovels, rakes, pruning saws, saws and hedge and brush trimmers, as well as power lawnmowers, tractors and spraying and dusting equipment.

***Required skills/personal attributes.*** Gardeners and groundskeepers should be responsible and able to work with little or no supervision. They also should be able to get along well with people. Groundskeepers who operate large tractors and other heavy equipment should have good driving records and ideally some experience driving a truck.

***Work environment.*** Although many gardening jobs are seasonal, involving spring and summer cleanup, planting, mowing and trimming, gardeners and groundskeepers work outdoors in all kinds of weather. They must frequently complete jobs in time for scheduled events, such as funerals. They work with pesticides, insecticides and other potentially hazardous chemicals, as well as dangerous equipment, such as chain saws and electric clippers.

***Education/training/certification.*** Most gardeners and groundskeepers are high school graduates. Some gain experience as home gardeners or working in nurseries. There are no national standards for gardeners, although some states require certification for workers who use chemicals extensively.

There are many two- to four-year programs in landscape management, interiorscape and ornamental horticulture. The Professional Grounds Management Society awards certification to managers with a combination of eight years of experience and formal education beyond high school.

***Salary range.*** In 1990, gardeners and groundskeepers earned from $170 to $450 a week. The average hourly rate for seasonal laborers was about $6.10; for year-round laborers, about $7.33; and for supervisors, about $9.40. Managers with a four-year degree earned about $34,292 a year.

***Opportunities for advancement/career growth.*** A gardener or groundskeeper may advance to supervisor, then to grounds manager or superintendent. Many become landscape contractors.

Employment opportunities for gardeners and groundskeepers are expected to increase much faster than in other occupations, reflecting a rise in construction of commercial and industrial properties. Developers will continue to seek out interior and exterior landscaping services in an effort to attract prospective buyers. The owners of existing buildings are expected to upgrade lawn and landscaping to maintain tenants. More two-income families are opting to employ lawn maintenance and landscaping services to enhance their property value and conserve their leisure time.

***Drawbacks for part-timers.*** The pay is low for the average gardener and the work can be physically demanding.

***Advantages for part-timers.*** About one out of three gardeners and groundskeepers works part-time. Jobs should be plentiful for students working their way through school, as well as older workers looking for part-time employment during retirement. One out of five gardeners is self-employed, providing landscape maintenance directly to customers on a contractual basis.

***For more information.*** Write to the Associated Landscape Contractors of America, Inc., 405 N. Washington St., Suite 104, Falls Church, VA 22046.

# HOMEMAKER-HOME HEALTH AIDES

**Homemaker-home health aides** help elderly, disabled and ill people live comfortably in their own homes rather than in institutions, such as nursing homes. For each client, they have detailed instructions explaining when to visit and which services to perform.

Some aides care for small children when a parent is incapacitated. Others help patients recently discharged from the hospital with short-term needs, such as housekeeping, shopping and preparing meals. Daily personal care may include bathing, hair care, help with prescribed exercises and changing dressings.

Working under the supervision of a registered nurse, physical therapist or social worker, aides report changes in each patient's condition and participate in reviewing cases with a care team of registered nurses, therapists and other health professionals.

***Required skills/personal attributes.*** Homemaker-home health aides should be in good health, with the strength and stamina to lift and move equipment and patients. They should have good communication skills and be patient and compassionate.

***Work environment.*** While they may go to the same home everyday for months or years, it is more common for homemaker-home health aides to visit as many as five different patients in a single day. Most aides spend a good portion of the day traveling from client to client and to routine visits with supervisors.

***Education/training/certification.*** Training requirements are changing with new federal guidelines. Homemaker-home health aides whose employers receive reimbursement from Medicare must complete at least 75 hours of classroom and practical training supervised by a registered nurse, and pass a competency test covering 12 areas. Training and testing programs may be offered by the employing agency and may vary depending on state regulations. Some states require aides to pass a physical examination.

The National HomeCaring Council, part of the Foundation for Hospice and Home Care, offers a voluntary National Homemaker-Home Health Aide certification.

*Salary range.* Some homemaker-home health aides earn minimum wage. In larger cities, they may earn up to $10 an hour only for time worked in the home. They are not paid for time spent traveling from home to home.

*Opportunities for advancement/career growth.* Advancement is limited. The most experienced aides assist with medical equipment. Most employers give small pay increases as aides gain experience and take on additional responsibilities. Employment for homemaker-home health aides is expected to grow much faster than the average occupation throughout the '90s. This reflects an aging population as well as an increasing reliance on home care.

*Drawbacks for part-timers.* Public and private funding may affect job availability, although prospects currently look excellent. Low pay and emotional demands of the job leads to high turnover.

*Advantages for part-timers.* While most homemaker-home health aides are employed by home health agencies, visiting nurse associations, hospitals, public health and welfare departments and temporary help firms, self-employed aides are free to accept clients, set fees and arrange schedules. There is an increased demand for male aides with the continued spread of AIDS among gay men.

*For more information.* Write to the Foundation for Hospice and Homecare/National HomeCaring Council, 519 C St. NE, Washington, DC 20002.

# LICENSED PRACTICAL NURSES (LPNs)

Licensed practical nurses care for sick, injured, convalescing and handicapped patients under the direction of physicians and registered nurses. In hospitals and nursing homes, they provide basic bedside care. They monitor vital signs, such as temperature and blood pressure. They may also treat bedsores, give injections and enemas, apply dressings, give alcohol rubs and massages, apply ice packs and insert catheters. Most LPNs also bathe, dress, feed and care for the emotional needs of patients. Some may be licensed to administer medicines or start intravenous fluids, help deliver babies or supervise nursing assistants and aides.

In doctors' offices and clinics, LPNs may set appointments, keep records and perform other clerical duties. In the home, they may prepare meals and teach family members simple nursing tasks.

***Required skills/personal attributes.*** LPNs should be sympathetic and emotionally stable. They must be able to follow orders and work under close supervision.

***Work environment.*** In hospitals, nursing homes and private homes, LPNs often work long or irregular hours to provide around-the-clock care. They stand for long periods of time and help patients move in bed, stand or walk. Caring for sick, confused and uncooperative patients and their families is often stressful. In hospitals, LPNs may be exposed to caustic chemicals, shock from electrical equipment and infectious diseases.

***Education/training/certification.*** All states require LPNs to pass a licensing examination after completing a state-approved practical nursing program. A high school diploma is usually required for entry into one-year programs offered by trade and technical-vocational schools and some hospitals. Two-year community and junior colleges and four-year schools also offer training. Most programs include classroom study and supervised clinical practice.

***Salary range.*** In 1990, full-time LPNs earned from $312 to $539 a week. Part-timers averaged about $10.70 an hour.

***Opportunities for advancement/career growth.*** The demand for LPNs is expected to increase significantly in the '90s in response to the long-term health care needs of an aging population. Nursing homes will offer most new jobs. There should also be rapid growth in residential care facilities, such as board and care homes, group homes for the handicapped and in-home care.

Hospitals facing a scarcity of registered nurses (RNs) as well as physicians working in clinics and those in private practice also should hire more LPNs.

***Drawbacks for part-timers.*** None.

***Advantages for part-timers.*** About a quarter of all LPNs work part-time. Some work for temporary help agencies. Private duty nursing affords a great deal of freedom in setting work hours.

***For more information.*** Write to the Communications Department, National League of Nursing, 350 Hudson St., New York, NY 10014.

# MANAGEMENT CONSULTANTS

Public and private organizations hire management consultants to solve a range of business problems when they lack internal resources or need expertise. Some consultants work alone. Others join a team of consultants.

In general, management consultants collect, review and analyze information, such as annual revenues. They may interview employees and spend time observing operations. Consultants make recommendations that are appropriate to the general nature of the business, its relation to competitors and its internal organization. After presenting their recommendations to the client in an oral presentation and written report, many management consultants assist in implementing their proposal.

Management consultants working in government are often called **management analysts**.

***Required skills/personal attributes.*** Management consultants should be self-motivated and able to work with little supervision. To develop creative solutions to a variety of business problems, they need strong analytical, oral and written communication skills, along with good judgment. The ability to manage time effectively is essential. Self-employed consultants must be organized, have strong marketing skills and several years of consulting experience.

***Work environment.*** Management consultants usually divide their time between their office and a client's operation. Much of their time is spent indoors in clean, well-lighted offices. Working in a client's production facility may mean less-favorable conditions. Frequent travel and deadlines often call for long hours.

***Education/training/certification.*** Employers and clients in private industry prefer to hire consultants with MBAs or master's degrees in a specialized area, such as computers, information sciences or engineering, and several years of related experience. Government agencies hire management analysts with bachelor's degrees and no work experience at entry-level, and provide formal classroom training.

Most consultants routinely attend conferences to stay up-to-date on developments in their fields. The Institute of Management Consultants (a division of the Council of Consulting Organizations) offers a voluntary Certified Management Consultant (CMC) designation to those who pass an examination and meet minimum levels of education and experience.

***Salary range.*** Most consulting services are provided on a contractual basis. In 1990, earnings ranged from $39,900 to $200,000 or more per year for partners in firms and entrepreneurs.

***Opportunities for advancement/career growth.*** Employment for consultants looks very bright into the '90s as private industry and government agencies look for ways to reduce costs and improve performance. Growth is anticipated to be especially strong for consulting firms and individuals who can fill specialized needs in emerging niches, such as biotechnology.

***Drawbacks for part-timers.*** The livelihood of a management consultant depends on his or her ability to maintain and expand a client base, which can be challenging at times. Competition for jobs is expected to be keen in the private sector.

***Advantages for part-timers.*** Self-employed consultants can often set their own hours and work at home. Those with MBAs, a strong human resources background, or who have expertise in an emerging area, such as biotechnology, will be in demand.

***For more information.*** Write to the Council of Consulting Organizations, Inc., 251 Fifth Avenue, New York, NY 10175.

# MEDICAL RECORD TECHNICIANS

Medical record technicians organize and evaluate the records that health care professionals use in treating patients. After ensuring that a patient's medical chart is complete, they verify that all forms are present, properly identified and signed and that all necessary information is on computer file.

Medical record technicians assign a standard code to each diagnosis and procedure. They may use a packaged computer program to assign a patient to one of several hundred "diagnosis-related groups" or DRGs. This classification determines the amount the hospital will be reimbursed if the patient is covered by Medicare or other insurance companies. Some medical record technicians tabulate and analyze data to help improve patient care, control costs and respond to surveys.

***Required skills/personal attributes.*** Medical record technicians should have good communications skills and a good memory. The ability to concentrate and attention to detail are essential. Computer literacy is helpful.

***Work environment.*** Medical record technicians work in pleasant, comfortable offices. They have little contact with patients. Because they work at computer terminals for prolonged periods, they may be prone to eyestrain and/or muscle pain.

***Education/training/certification.*** Medical record technicians may complete a two-year associate degree program through a community or junior college or an independent study program in Medical Record Technology offered by the American Medical Record Association (AMRA).

Most employers prefer to hire accredited record technicians (ARTs). Applicants with an associate degree from a program accredited by the Committee on Allied Health Education and Accreditation (CAHEA) of the American Medical Association, or who have successfully completed the independent study program in Medical Record Technology must pass a written examination offered by the American Medical Record Association.

***Salary range.*** In 1991, full-time medical record technicians working in hospitals earned from $8.70 to $13.08 an hour.

***Opportunities for advancement/career growth.*** In medium or large facilities, medical record technicians may specialize in one aspect of medical records, or they may supervise medical record clerks and transcriptionists. With experience, senior staff members may advance to management as medical record administrators, assistant directors or directors of a medical record department.

Job prospects should be excellent for medical record technicians throughout the '90s because of an increasing number of medical tests, treatments and procedures required by an aging population. In addition, medical records will increasingly be scrutinized by third-party payers, courts and consumers.

Although hospitals will continue to employ most medical record technicians, there should be rapid growth in large medical records practices and offices in response to changes in Medicare policies. Growth will also be seen in Health Management Organizations (HMOs), nursing homes and home health agencies.

***Drawbacks for part-timers.*** Most medical record technicians work full-time in hospitals, where departments are open 18 to 24 hours a day.

***Advantages for part-timers.*** Some medical record technicians are self-employed as consultants to nursing homes and physicians' offices. Others may be able to negotiate flexible hours working for insurance companies, accounting and law firms that deal with health matters.

***For more information.*** Write to the American Medical Record Association, 919 N. Michigan Ave., Suite 1400, Chicago, IL 60611.

# NUCLEAR MEDICINE TECHNOLOGISTS

In this branch of radiology, nuclear medicine technologists use radionuclides—unstable atoms that emit radiation spontaneously—that physicians use to diagnose and treat diseases. After administering the correct dosage of radiopharmaceuticals to patients, nuclear medicine technologists monitor the function of tissues and organs using a gamma scintillation camera or by looking for abnormal concentrations of radioactivity on a computer screen. They also may relay the results to physicians via film output.

Nuclear medicine technologists also perform clinical laboratory procedures, called radioimmunoassay studies, to assess the behavior of the radioactive substance inside the body. They keep accurate records of radionuclides used on each patient, as well as how all radioactive materials are used and disposed of.

***Required skills/personal attributes.*** Nuclear medicine technologists should have good interpersonal skills. They should be detail-oriented and skilled in chemistry as well as the operation of electronic equipment and computers. They also need physical stamina and strength for work that requires prolonged standing, moving and turning patients who are sick or disabled.

***Work environment.*** Nine out of 10 nuclear medicine technologists work in comfortable, well-lighted departments of hospitals. Some work in physicians' offices and clinics. In addition to wearing badges to measure radiation level, they use shields, syringes, gloves and other protective devices to minimize the potential for exposure.

***Education/training/certification.*** The Committee on Allied Health Education and Accreditation (CAHEA) sanctions most formal training programs. Two-year certificate programs are generally offered in hospitals. Two-year associate degrees are offered by community colleges, and four-year schools offer bachelor's degrees.

Individuals with science backgrounds, especially radiologic and ultrasound technologists, may specialize in nuclear medicine by completing a one-year certificate program. All nuclear technologists must meet minimum federal standards for administration of radioactive drugs and operation of equipment. About half of all states require nuclear medicine technologists to be licensed.

Voluntary certification or registration is available from the American Registry of Radiologic Technologists (ARRT) and from the Nuclear Medicine Technology Certification Board (NMTCB).

***Salary range.*** Salaries for full-time nuclear medicine technologists working in hospitals range from $23,925 to $34,247.

***Opportunities for advancement/career growth.*** Nuclear medicine technologists may advance to supervisor, chief technologist and finally department administrator or director. Some specialize in a clinical area, such as nuclear cardiology or computer analysis. Others leave patient care to take positions in research laboratories. Job prospects are bright as the population ages, and technological innovations promise to increase the diagnostic uses of nuclear medicine to detect cancer and other diseases at earlier stages. Reports of shortages are widespread.

***Drawbacks for part-timers.*** Most technologists employed in hospitals work full-time and may be on-call on a rotational basis.

***Advantages for part-timers.*** Opportunities for part-time and shift work are available. Technologists working in physicians' offices and diagnostic imaging centers or as instructors may be able to negotiate flexible schedules or part-time employment.

***For more information.*** Write to the Society of Nuclear Medicine-Technologist Section, 136 Madison Ave., New York, NY 10016.

# OCCUPATIONAL THERAPISTS

Occupational therapists help individuals with mental, physical, developmental and emotional disabilities develop and maintain the skills necessary to live independent, productive and satisfying lives.

With the help of an occupational therapist, even patients who lack basic motor function and reasoning abilities can learn to compensate through a variety of activities designed to increase manual dexterity, visual acuity and recall. Therapists begin by helping patients take care of their daily needs. From there, patients can steadily progress to finding and holding a job.

Using computer programs, therapists can help patients improve decision-making, abstract reasoning, problem-solving and perceptual skills. They also provide adaptive equipment for patients with permanent functional disabilities. Microprocessor devices, for example, may permit individuals with severe limitations to walk or talk.

Occupational therapists also help mentally handicapped people and recovering alcoholics cope with the tasks of daily life, such as budgeting, shopping and using public transportation.

***Required skills/personal attributes.*** Occupational therapists should be patient. Ingenuity and imagination help them adapt activities to individual needs in a variety of home and work settings.

***Work environment.*** In large rehabilitation centers, therapists often work in spacious rooms with kitchen areas. Most therapists spend a large part of their working hours on their feet and have to lift and move patients. Those providing home health care may spend several hours a day driving from appointment to appointment.

***Education/training/certification.*** In addition to a bachelor's degree in occupational therapy from an accredited school, occupational therapists in most states must be licensed. Those candidates who pass the national certification examination given by the American Occupational Therapy Certification Board are awarded the title of Registered Occupational Therapist. In addition to course work including physical, biological and behavioral sciences, therapists must complete six months of supervised clinical internship.

***Salary range.*** In 1990, full-time occupational therapists working in hospitals and medical schools earned from $26,500 to $38,500 per year.

***Opportunities for advancement/career growth.*** While most jobs are found in hospitals, rehabilitation centers and psychiatric facilities, many occupational therapists work in school systems, nursing homes, community mental health centers, adult day-care programs, outpatient clinics and residential care facilities.

Employment opportunities are expected to increase much faster than average. In addition, medical advances continue to make it possible for more patients with critical health problems to survive, with extensive therapy. More people reaching middle age will suffer heart attacks and strokes. Additional services will be required for disabled patients who are 75 and older.

***Drawbacks for part-timers.*** None.

***Advantages for part-timers.*** A small, but rapidly growing, number of occupational therapists are in private practice. Some are solo practitioners, while others work in group practice. These self-employed therapists see patients referred by physicians and provide contract and consulting services to nursing homes, adult day-care and home health agencies.

***For more information.*** Write to the American Occupational Therapy Association, P.O. Box 1725, 1383 Piccard Dr., Rockville, MD 20849.

# OPHTHALMIC LABORATORY TECHNICIANS

Ophthalmic laboratory technicians make prescription eyeglass lenses or manufacture lenses for other optical instruments, such as telescopes and binoculars. Using prescription specifications provided by dispensing opticians, optometrists or ophthalmologists, technicians cut, grind, edge and finish lenses and then assemble them in frames to provide finished glasses.

***Required skills/personal attributes.*** Ophthalmic laboratory technicians need a knowledge of science and math, as well as manual dexterity and visual acuity for precision work.

**Work environment.** Ophthalmic labs are relatively quiet, clean and well-lighted. Technicians have limited contact with the public they serve. They spend a great deal of time standing and may wear goggles to protect their eyes from flying glass and chemical solutions.

**Education/training/certification.** High school graduates may learn necessary skills on the job. Depending on aptitude, it can take six to 18 months to become proficient in all phases of the work. Some technicians learn their trade in the armed forces. Others attend a small number of programs in optical technology offered by vocational-technical institutes or trade schools. Programs vary in length from six months to a year, and award certificates or diplomas.

**Salary range.** In 1991, skilled technicians earned between $12,000 and $17,000. Trainees may start at minimum wage.

**Opportunities for advancement/career growth.** Employment opportunities are expected to increase much faster than the average for most occupations to meet the needs of an aging population and provide eyeglasses as a fashion item.

Most new jobs will be in retail chains that manufacture prescription glasses on the premises and provide fast service. Optical goods store chains, independent retailers, optical labs and ophthalmologists and optometrists also employ skilled technicians.

In small labs, technicians generally handle every phase of operation. In larger labs, they may specialize in one or more steps to form an assembly line. Technicians can advance to supervisor or manager. Some become dispensing opticians with further training or education.

**Drawbacks for part-timers.** Shifts in retail stores that advertise fast service and are open long hours may be full-time. Although job-sharing along an assembly line may be possible.

**Advantages for part-timers.** Technicians may be able to negotiate flexible hours if they work in the office of an ophthalmologist or optometrist where patient visits are scheduled ahead of time.

**For more information.** Write to the Commission on Opticiancy Accreditation, 10111 Martin Luther King Jr. Hwy., Suite 100, Bowie, MD 20720.

# PARALEGALS

Paralegals work "behind the scenes" to perform many of the same functions lawyers do. To help prepare a case for trial, they investigate facts to make sure all relevant information is uncovered. They may research appropriate laws, judicial decisions, legal articles and other materials to determine whether a client has a good case. Written reports, files and documents prepared by paralegals guide lawyers in preparing legal arguments. Paralegals may also draft pleadings to be filed in court, obtain affidavits and assist lawyers during trial.

Paralegals working in large, departmentalized law firms may specialize in an area such as bankruptcy, corporate law or real estate. In small and medium-sized law firms, they may handle duties that require general knowledge of many areas of law.

In government, duties vary according to the agency. Generally, paralegals analyze information for internal use and prepare informative and explanatory information on the law and agency regulations. Working for community legal service projects, they help clients who cannot afford legal aid.

A paralegal cannot accept clients, set legal fees, give legal advice or present a case in court.

***Required skills/personal attributes.*** Paralegals must be able to think logically and communicate their findings and opinions effectively, both orally and in writing. A thorough understanding of legal terminology and good research and investigative skills are essential. Paralegals are expected to have high ethical standards and stay abreast of new developments in the law that affect their areas of practice. As specialized software packages are increasingly used to search legal literature, organize and index materials and prepare tax computations, paralegals are expected to be computer literate.

***Work environment.*** Most paralegals work in offices and law libraries. Occasionally they will travel to gather information and perform other duties.

***Education/training/certification.*** While some employers offer on-the-job training, most prefer to hire paralegals with formal training in a specialized area of law and experience in a field useful to the firm. Training programs are offered by four-year colleges and universities and law schools, as well as community and junior colleges, business schools and proprietary schools.

The National Association of Legal Assistants has established standards for voluntary certification that require various combinations of education and experience. Applicants must complete a two-day examination administered yearly by the Certifying Board of Legal Assistants of the National Association of Legal Assistants. The designation Certified Legal Assistant (CLA) is a sign of competence that may increase employment and advancement opportunities.

***Salary range.*** Earnings vary widely, depending on training and experience as well as the employer and location. In 1991, full-time paralegals earned from $20,000 to $29,000 a year. Paralegals working for government agencies earned an average $32,164.

***Opportunities for advancement/career growth.*** Paralegals are usually entrusted with progressively more responsible duties and require less supervision. With experience, they may be promoted to supervise other paralegals and clerical staff and delegate work in large firms and government agencies. Others may prefer to move to other firms for advancement.

Job prospects look good for graduates of highly regarded formal programs. Job opportunities are expected to expand throughout the private sector and in community legal service programs as managers look for ways to cut legal costs and deal with emerging laws and judicial interpretations of existing laws.

***Drawbacks for part-timers.*** Competition may be keen. Paralegals tend to work a standard 40-hour week in corporations and government agencies, and longer hours in law firms.

***Advantages for part-timers.*** Some paralegals are self-employed and many are employed on a temporary basis during busy times of year.

***For more information.*** Write to the National Association of Legal Assistants, Inc., 1601 South Main St., Tulsa, OK 74119.

# PHOTOGRAPHERS

Photographers use technical and artistic skill to capture images of people, places and events that sell products, highlight news stories and bring back memories. Using a variety of cameras that can accept lenses designed for close-up, medium-range or distance photography, photographers make adjustments to control lighting and create a special mood or moment on film. They also depend on equipment and accessories—from colored filters to tripods to special lighting Photographers may develop and print their own photographs or send them to a photo lab for processing.

Photographers specialize in different areas. Many portrait photographers own their businesses and arrange for advertising, schedule appointments, and mount and frame pictures. Some self-employed photographers contract with stock photo agencies that grant magazines and other customers the rights to use photos for a fee.

**Commercial, editorial and industrial photographers** take photographs of products, buildings and groups of executives for annual reports, advertisements and catalogs. **Scientific photographers** illustrate and document research for reports and textbooks. **Photojournalists** record newsworthy events, people and places for newspapers, journals and magazines.

***Required skills/personal attributes.*** In addition to imagination and creativity, photographers need good eyesight, manual dexterity and technical expertise. They should be patient and enjoy working with detail. A knowledge of mathematics, physics and chemistry is also helpful. Photographers who use models and clients as subjects need good interpersonal skills. Those who are self-employed need good business skills to find clients, bill for jobs and keep accurate financial records.

***Work environment.*** Portrait work is often done in well-lighted, and ventilated studios. Some local travel may be necessary to take photographs in churches, synagogues and homes, or even internationally to take news photos. Photographers often stand or walk for long periods carrying heavy equipment. Those who develop and print their own work may spend long hours in cramped darkrooms. Many photographers put in long hours to meet deadlines.

***Education/training/certification:*** Many entry-level jobs require little formal preparation. Fashion, commercial and portrait photographers often learn on the job. As photography assistants, they set up lights, mix chemicals and develop and print film. Photojournalists, scientific and technical photographers usually require a college degree.

Colleges, universities, community and junior colleges, vocational-technical institutes, private trade and technical schools all offer courses in photography as part of communications or journalism programs. Art schools offer courses in design and composition.

***Salary range.*** In 1991, salaried photographers earned from $24,814 to $37,273. Some self-employed photographers earn more.

***Opportunities for advancement/career growth.*** Magazine and news photographers can head up graphic arts departments and become photo editors. The growing importance of visual images in education, communications, entertainment, marketing and research and development will open up opportunities for talented, hardworking photographers.

***Drawbacks for part-timers.*** Only the most skilled photographers with business ability are able to attract enough work to support themselves. Newspaper photographers work long, irregular hours. Finding clients can be time-consuming and stressful for self-employed photographers. Very few are successful enough to support themselves solely through their profession.

***Advantages for part-timers.*** Nearly half of all photographers are self-employed, and able to work flexible hours often out of their homes. Some contract with ad agencies, magazines and businesses to handle individual projects. Others operate portrait studios and provide photos to stock agencies. Some become "weekenders," supplementing a full-time income with part-time assignments taking wedding photos or portraits.

***For more information.*** Write to Professional Photographers of America, Inc., 1090 Executive Way, Des Plaines, IL  60018.

# PHYSICAL THERAPISTS

Physical therapists help people with injuries, diseases, burns and arthritis to relieve pain, improve mobility and prevent or limit permanent physical disability.

After evaluating a patient's medical history, therapists test and measure strength and range of motion. They develop written treatment plans and conduct periodic reevaluations as treatment progresses, modifying treatment if necessary.

Beginning with a technique called passive exercise, physical therapists work on increasing flexibility by stretching and manipulating a patient's joints and muscles. Later, weights and other exercises are added to the regimen to progressively improve strength, balance, coordination and endurance.

Sometimes electricity, heat and ultrasound are used to relieve pain and improve the condition of muscles. Other treatments include cold, water, traction and deep tissue massage.

As part of treatment, physical therapists motivate patients to use crutches, prostheses and wheelchairs to aid them in performing day-to-day activities. Some therapists specialize in pediatrics, geriatrics, sports therapy or other specialized areas.

***Required skills/personal attributes.*** Physical therapists should enjoy working with people. They need patience, tact and resourcefulness to motivate a variety of patients. They should be persistent and emotionally stable. Manual dexterity and physical stamina are essential.

***Work environment.*** Most physical therapists work in hospitals, clinics and offices that have been specially equipped. They may also travel to hospital rooms, homes and schools. The work can require stooping, kneeling, crouching, lifting and long periods of standing. They may also move heavy equipment.

***Education/training/certification.*** A bachelor's degree is often acceptable, but many employers now look for a master's degree, in addition to supervised clinical experience. Course work includes chemistry, anatomy and physiology. All states require physical therapists to be licensed. Candidates must be graduates of an accredited physical therapy program and pass an examination.

*Salary range.* Full-time physical therapists working in private hospitals earn from $14.83 to $20.52 an hour.

*Opportunities for advancement/career growth.* Prospects look very bright for physical therapists as new medical technologies continue to save more accident victims and newborns with birth defects. In addition, an aging population will become increasingly vulnerable to heart attacks, strokes and chronic debilitating conditions.

*Drawbacks for part-timers.* None.

*Advantages for part-timers.* One out of four physical therapists works part-time. Some are self-employed as solo practitioners or in group practice.

*For more information.* Write to the American Physical Therapy Association, 1111 North Fairfax Ave., Alexandria, VA 22314.

# PHYSICIAN'S ASSISTANTS

Physician's assistants, or PAs, are trained to perform many of the routine, but time-consuming tasks traditionally handled by physicians. They take medical histories, perform physical examinations, order laboratory tests and x-rays, make preliminary diagnoses and give inoculations. PAs are also trained to treat minor injuries by suturing, splinting and casting. In 30 states and the District of Columbia, they may prescribe medications.

PAs with managerial duties may oversee technicians and assistants. Others make house calls or go on rounds in hospitals. They often assist in specialty areas, such as family practice, internal medicine, emergency medicine and pediatrics.

***Required skills/personal attributes.*** PAs should demonstrate leadership, self-confidence and emotional stability.

***Work environment.*** PAs generally work in climate-controlled, well-lighted environments. Many do a lot of walking.

***Education/training/certification.*** Almost all states require new PAs to complete an accredited training program. Many programs require two years of college and some work experience and award a certificate, associate, bachelor's or master's degree. In 45 states, PAs must pass a certifying exam. In some states, the duties of the PA are determined by the supervising physician. In others, by the state's regulatory agency. All PAs should study throughout their careers to keep up with medical advances.

***Salary range.*** In 1991, full-time PAs working in hospitals and medical schools earned from $40,000 to $44,999. Earnings are slightly lower for PAs working for the federal government.

***Opportunities for advancement/career growth.*** Opportunities are expected to be excellent for PAs throughout the '90s—especially for those working in rural and inner-city clinics that have difficulty attracting physicians. The anticipated expansion of health services, such as HMOs and group medical practices, and growing emphasis on cost containment should lead to more jobs for PAs.

***Drawbacks for part-timers.*** In some environments, PAs may be expected to work long or irregular hours. Emergency room PAs may work two 24-hour shifts a week. Others may work three 12-hour shifts a week.

***Advantages for part-timers.*** Although physicians' offices may require work at night and on weekends, PAs should be able to more easily negotiate part-time schedules. Other opportunities are in clinics, public health clinics and rehabilitation centers with regular business hours.

***For more information.*** Write to the American Academy of Physician Assistants, 950 North Washington St., Alexandria, VA 22314.

# PRESCHOOL WORKERS

Preschool workers teach and care for children under the age of 5 in day-care centers, preschools and family day-care homes. They play a role in helping children explore their interests, develop talents and independence, and build self-confidence and social skills.

Depending on their experience and educational background, some workers are also responsible for organizing a range of activities that stimulate physical, emotional, intellectual and social growth. Most capitalize on play to further language development through storytelling, improve social skills and introduce scientific and mathematical concepts.

Most preschool workers keep careful records of each child's progress and discuss with parents. Daily and long-term schedules of activities are designed to balance quiet and active time.

***Required skills/personal attributes.*** Preschool workers should be enthusiastic, fair and able to deal with disruptive children. Patience and physical stamina are essential. Skills in music, art and storytelling are important. Organizational, management and administrative skills are helpful, especially for the self-employed workers.

***Work environment.*** Preschool workers work in cheerful, comfortable homes, schools, religious institutions or private buildings. Those who provide care in their own homes are generally called family day-care providers. Although the work is rewarding, it can also be physically and emotionally taxing. Most preschool workers are constantly bending, stooping and lifting.

***Education/training/certification.*** Many states regulate training for preschool workers. Although some need only a high school diploma, many earn college degrees in child development or early childhood education.

Many states require a Child Development Associate (CDA) credential, awarded by the Council for Early Childhood Professional Recognition. Applicants must complete a training and assessment program and demonstrate requisite skills and knowledge.

*Salary range.* In 1990, full-time preschool workers earned about $200 a week. Earnings of self-employed workers vary according to the number of hours worked, the number and ages of children in care and the geographic location.

*Opportunities for advancement/career growth.* With experience, preschool workers may advance to supervisory or administrative positions in large childcare centers or preschools. Advancement often requires additional training. With a bachelor's degree, workers can become certified to teach in public school at the kindergarten, elementary and secondary levels. Some start their own businesses.

Employment opportunities are projected to increase much faster than average because of an increase in the number of children under 5 with two working parents. Trends show that many women are returning to work sooner after childbirth.

*Drawbacks for part-timers.* Pay is generally low.

*Advantages for part-timers.* Part-time workers may arrange to work staggered shifts to cover the long day in day-care centers. Public preschools may operate only nine or 10 months of the year. Family day-care providers have flexible hours, but may work long or unusual hours to fit parents' schedules. About half of all preschool workers are self-employed as family day-care providers.

*For more information.* Write to the American Federation of Teachers, Organizing Department, 555 New Jersey Ave. NW, Washington, DC 20001.

## PSYCHOLOGISTS

Psychologists study human behavior and mental processes to understand, explain and change people's behavior. **Research psychologists** investigate the physical, cognitive, emotional or social aspects of human behavior.

Psychologists may focus on any of a number of applied fields. **Educational psychologists** design, develop and evaluate educational programs. **Developmental psychologists** study developmental patterns and behavior from infancy to adulthood. **Organizational psychologists** work with personnel, administration and management in large organizations. Other psychologists specialize in providing services to specialized populations, such as cancer patients or families. Many counsel individuals in a series of ongoing sessions. Others conduct group therapy sessions and design and monitor behavior modification programs.

***Required skills/personal attributes.*** To deal effectively with a wide range of troubled people, psychologists should be emotionally stable, patient, sensitive and compassionate. They should have good verbal and writing skills and be able to lead and inspire others. Because computers are widely used to record and analyze information, computer literacy is a plus.

***Work environment.*** A psychologist's specialty often determines the work setting. Psychologists who counsel individuals in private practice have pleasant, comfortable offices and have flexible hours. Those employed in hospitals, nursing homes and other health facilities often work in less-appealing environments and may put in evenings and weekends.

***Education/training/certification.*** Psychologists who counsel patients in private practice or clinical settings must have either a Ph.D. or a Doctor of Psychology (Psy.D.).

Those who earn a master's degree may administer and interpret tests and conduct research and counsel patients under supervision.

A bachelor's degree qualifies candidate to assist psychologists and other professionals in community mental health centers, vocational rehabilitation offices and correctional programs, or work as trainees in government or business. But opportunities for advancement are limited.

Psychologists who work in private practice or offer any type of patient care must be licensed by the state. Requirements vary, but most states require a doctoral degree, up to two years of professional experience and a passing grade on a standardized written examination. Some states require candidates to complete additional oral or essay examinations.

Some states require continuing education for relicensure.

***Salary range.*** In 1989, psychologists with a doctoral degree earned from $55,000 to $67,000. Those in private practice and applied specialties can earn considerably more.

***Opportunities for advancement/career growth.*** Opportunities for psychologists are expected to grow throughout the '90s in response to a growing demand for programs that help people deal with alcohol and drug abuse, marital strife and family violence.

More companies will turn to psychologists who can design surveys, conduct personnel testing and statistical analysis, and evaluate programs.

Opportunities will be best for those with a doctoral degree from a leading university in an applied area, such as counseling. Most graduates with a master's degree will find the best opportunities in schools. Those holding only a bachelor's degree can expect few opportunities.

***Drawbacks for part-timers.*** Psychologists in private practice may have to work evening hours to accommodate clients. Those who work in hospitals, nursing homes and other health facilities often work evenings and weekends.

***Advantages for part-timers.*** Almost half of all psychologists are self-employed and can set their own hours. Those who work in schools may be able to take advantage of part-time and seasonal schedules.

***For more information.*** Write to the American Psychological Association, Educational Programs, 1200 17th St. NW, Washington, DC 20036.

# PUBLIC RELATIONS SPECIALISTS

Public relations specialists build and maintain positive relationships with the public as advocates for business, government, universities, hospitals, schools and other organizations. They often help management formulate a sound public relations policy.

They may tell an organization's "story" to customers or the general public through an annual report and other published materials that explain the organization's policies, activities and accomplishments. They often write press releases and contact people in the media who might print or broadcast information about the organization. They may also coordinate programs and special events, such as speaking engagements or slide presentations, to introduce the public to the organization and its representatives. In addition, they are responsible for establishing and maintaining cooperative relationships with representatives of community, consumer, employee and public interest groups, as well as print and broadcast journalists.

Public relations specialists working in government are sometimes called press secretaries or public affairs specialists. They keep the public informed about activities of government agencies or officials.

***Required skills/personal attributes.*** PR specialists should be able to write and speak well. They should be organized, detail-oriented and be able to work well with different types of people. Enthusiasm and stamina help them deal with hectic days and special events.

***Work environment.*** Most public relations specialists work in comfortable, well-lighted offices in management and public relations firms, educational institutions, hospitals and other service organizations. Some are self-employed and work at home. Deadlines and demanding clients can make work stressful. Frequent travel may be required to meet with clients and conduct events.

***Education/training/certification.*** A bachelor's degree in public relations, journalism or communications, combined with public relations experience gained through an internship, is considered excellent preparation for a career in public relations. Some employers and clients seek people with training or experience in fields related to their business, such in science, sales and finance.

***Salary range.*** In 1990, full-time salaried public relations specialists earned from $15,000 to $52,000 a year.

***Opportunities for advancement/career growth.*** In large organizations, the director of public relations is often also a vice president. Account executives and assistants write, prepare materials, maintain contacts and respond to inquiries.

Opportunities for employment will be good, especially in the areas of environmental and biotechnology.

***Drawbacks for part-timers.*** Because public relations specialists often handle a range of duties for more than one client, the pace and deadline pressure can become intense. Frequent overtime and long-distance travel may be required.

***Advantages for part-timers.*** The basic tasks involved for most projects are writing and telephoning and can easily be handled at home. Self-employed public relations specialists often have a lot of flexibility in setting their own schedules.

***For more information.*** Write to the Public Relations Society of America, Inc., 33 Irving Place, New York, NY 10003.

# RADIOLOGIC TECHNOLOGISTS

**Radiographers** produce "pictures" of parts of the human body using radiation, magnetic imaging, radio waves, sound waves and computers. These images are used by physicians to diagnose a range of medical problems. Radiographers work with x-rays, CT scans and magnetic resonance imaging (MRI).

**Radiation therapy technicians** administer a course of radiation treatment to cancer patients. **Sonographers** use non-ionizing ultrasound equipment to transit high frequency sound waves into areas of a patient's body. Reflected echoes form an image that can be viewed on screen, photographed or recorded on a print-out strip.

All radiologic technologists keep patient records and adjust and maintain equipment. Those with supervisory responsibilities prepare work schedules and evaluate equipment purchases.

***Required skills/personal attributes.*** Radiologic technologists should have good interpersonal skills. Attention to detail and skill in chemistry as well as the operation of electronic and computer equipment are essential. They also need stamina and strength as their work requires prolonged standing and frequent lifting.

***Work environment.*** Some radiologic technologists travel in mobile imaging vans. Radiation hazards are minimized by use of lead aprons, gloves and other shielding devices. Radiologic technologists are prone to emotional burnout from regularly treating very ill and dying patients.

***Education/training/certification.*** Hospitals prefer to hire technologists with formal training. Programs range in length from one to four years and lead to a certificate, associate degree or bachelor's degree. Two-year programs are most prevalent. A master's or bachelor's degree may be necessary for supervisory, administrative and teaching positions.

Many states require radiographers to be licensed, 20 require radiation therapy technologists to be licensed and one (Utah) licenses diagnostic medical sonographers.

Many employers prefer to hire registered technologists. Voluntary registration is offered by the American Registry of Radiologic Technologists (ARRT) in both radiography and radiation therapy. The American Registry of Diagnostic Medical Sonographers (ARDMS) certifies the competence of sonographers. To become registered, technologists must graduate from a school accredited by the Committee of Allied Health Education and Accreditation (CAHEA) or meet other prerequisites and pass a written examination.

***Salary range.*** In 1991, part-time radiologic technologists earned about $12.76 an hour. Diagnostic medical sonographers earned an average $15.18 an hour. Full-time radiation therapy technologists earned from $24,699 to $35,811 a year.

***Opportunities for advancement/career growth.*** Most radiologic technologists are radiographers. More than half work in hospitals. Others work in physicians' offices and clinics, including diagnostic imaging centers. With experience and additional training, staff technologists in large radiography departments may be promoted to perform special procedures, including CT scanning and ultrasound.

Employment opportunities are expected to grow much faster than the average, especially in physician offices and clinics. As technology continues to evolve, more uses will be found for this method of "safe" exploratory surgery and cancer treatment.

More technologists will work "on the road," traveling in mobile clinics to respond to needs of rural communities.

***Drawbacks for part-timers.*** None.

***Advantages for part-timers.*** Part-time work is widely available. Salaries and working conditions will continue to improve.

***For more information.*** Write to the Division of Allied Health Education and Accreditation, American Medical Association, 515 N. State St., Chicago, IL 60610.

# REAL ESTATE AGENTS/BROKERS

**Real estate agents** help clients find the neighborhood, home and financing that fit their needs and budgets. Agents help buyers and sellers negotiate fair prices and ensure that all special terms and conditions, such as inspections, are carried out before the closing date.

**Real estate brokers** market and sell real estate and may rent and manage properties for a fee. They often provide buyers with information about loans to finance a purchase.

Most agents and brokers sell residential property and obtain listings, or the agreement of homeowners to place properties for sale. A few large real estate firms or specialized agencies sell commercial, industrial or other types of property.

***Required skills/personal attributes.*** Personable, ambitious people who enjoy selling should have a good chance of success in real estate. Honesty, tact and an ability to motivate prospective buyers are important, as are organization, attention to detail and a good memory for names and faces. Computer literacy is also a plus.

**Work environment.** Real estate agents and brokers are generally based in offices, but spend much of their time showing properties to prospective buyers. They usually drive their own automobiles. Most real estate agencies are small. Larger agencies may have hundreds of agents operating out of many, small branch offices.

**Education/training/certification.** Real estate agents and brokers must be licensed in every state. High school graduates who are at least 18 may take the written examination, which is more comprehensive for brokers than for agents. Most states require candidates for the general sales license to complete at least 30 hours of classroom instruction. Those seeking the broker's license must complete 90 hours of formal training and have up to three years of experience selling real estate. Some states waive the experience requirement for a broker's license if applicants have a bachelor's degree in real estate.

A small but growing number of states require agents to have 60 hours of college credit, roughly the equivalent of an associate degree. State licenses generally must be renewed every one or two years. Many states require continuing education through the National Association of Realtors for license renewal.

**Salary range.** Most independent real estate agents provide services to a licensed broker on a contract basis in return for a portion of the commission earned from the sale of the property. The commission varies according to the type of property and its value. Commissions may be divided among several agents and brokers when one obtains the listing and another makes the sale. An agent's commission is about half the total amount received by firm.

In 1990, full-time real estate agents earned about $19,000 a year. Brokers earned about $55,000. Successful salespeople earn considerably more.

**Opportunities for advancement/career growth.** Formally trained real estate agents can advance to sales manager or general manager. Those with a broker's license may open their own offices. Some may become property or real estate managers or enter mortgage financing and real estate investment counseling. A maturing population will ensure a larger market for home purchases. As incomes rise, many people will invest in additional real estate.

***Drawbacks for part-timers.*** A beginner's earnings are often irregular for up to six months. A few brokers allow agents a draw against future earnings. But, especially during periods of tight credit, weeks or months may go by without a sale. Beginners may become discouraged and leave the profession.

***Advantages for part-timers.*** Many real estate agents and brokers work part-time. Most are self-employed and work flexible hours, although they may have to work some evenings and weekends to accommodate clients. Some leave and re-enter the profession depending on the strength of the market and personal circumstances.

***For more information.*** Write to the National Association of Realtors. 875 N. Michigan Ave., Chicago, IL 60611.

# RECEPTIONISTS

Receptionists work in almost every type of business. Often they are the first face a customer or visitor sees. They may give directions, answer questions and refer callers to the appropriate person. In hospitals and doctors' offices, receptionists may obtain personal and financial information from patients and direct them to the proper waiting room. In beauty shops, they set appointments. In factories, large business firms and government offices, they provide identification cards to visitors.

Many receptionists keep a master record of callers, including the time they arrived and who they visited. They also may perform clerical duties, such as typing, filing, opening and sorting mail and preparing travel vouchers. Increasingly, receptionists use automated office equipment, such as word processors or personal computers.

***Required skills/personal attributes.*** A receptionist should have a pleasant appearance, personality and voice. Good typing and other office skills are also important. Computer literacy is a plus.

***Work environment.*** Receptionists usually work in stylish, well-furnished and well-lighted reception areas. Although there may be a lot of traffic from visitors and employees, the area is typically quiet. Many tasks are repetitious. Depending on the business, the job may be stressful at times. But it is not physically demanding.

***Education/training/certification.*** Receptionists are typically trained on the job to use office equipment and forms as well how to interview clients.

***Salary range.*** In 1990, full-time receptionists earned about $270 a week. In 1991, the federal government paid beginning receptionists with a high school diploma and six months of experience about $12,400.

***Opportunities for advancement/career growth.*** Employment opportunities for receptionists are expected to grow much faster than average, especially in doctors' and dentists' offices, law firms, temporary help agencies and consulting firms. Many receptionists transfer to other occupations for career advancement and better pay.

***Drawbacks for part-timers.*** Pay is low and opportunities for advancement are limited.

***Advantages for part-timers.*** One out of three receptionists works part-time, and job-sharing is common.

***For more information.*** Contact local service companies or temporary help agencies for information about job opportunities.

# RECREATION THERAPISTS

Recreation therapists use medically approved activities to enhance and maintain a patient's physical, mental and emotional well-being. These activities may include sports and games, dance, drama, art, music—even field trips.

In clinical settings, such as hospitals and rehabilitation centers, therapists work in cooperation with physicians, nurses, psychologists, social workers and physical and occupational therapists to develop therapeutic activity programs consistent with a patient's medical needs and interests. In nursing homes, residential facilities and community recreation departments, they are often known as activity directors. They offer elderly and disabled people opportunities for regular exercise, mental stimulation and social contact.

***Required skills/personal attributes.*** Recreation therapists should enjoy working with disabled people and be patient, tactful and imaginative in adapting activities to individual needs. Stamina and good physical coordination are important.

***Work environment.*** Although they may plan events and keep records in an office, recreation therapists spend most of their time in special activity or recreation rooms, or outside, on playing fields and in swimming pools. They often lift and carry equipment and participate in activities.

***Education/training/certification.*** A bachelor's degree in therapeutic recreation is usually required by hospitals and other clinical employers. An associate degree in recreation therapy, training in art, drama or music or related work experience may be sufficient for activity directors in nursing homes.

A few states license recreation therapists. Applicants must pass an examination after graduating from an accredited program. The National Council for Therapeutic Recreation Certification certifies therapeutic recreation specialists, and therapeutic recreation assistants. Applicants must have a bachelor's degree and 360 hours of internship under the supervision of a certified therapeutic recreation specialist, and pass a written examination.

***Salary range.*** In 1990, full-time recreation therapists working in nursing homes earned from $15,000 to $25,000 per year.

***Opportunities for advancement/career growth.*** The growing need for long-term care as well as physical and psychiatric services throughout the '90s promises many opportunities for recreation therapists. New jobs will be created in hospitals, adult day-care centers and outpatient programs, units offering short-term mental health care and alcohol and drug abuse programs. Long-term rehabilitation and psychiatric hospitals also will offer opportunities.

***Drawbacks for part-timers.*** The pay is low, especially for less than full-time work.

***Advantages for part-timers.*** Some recreation therapists are self-employed and contract with nursing homes or community agencies to develop and oversee programs.

***For more information.*** Write to the American Therapeutic Recreation Association, C.O. Associated Management Systems, P.O. Box 15215, Hattiesburg, MS 39402.

# REGISTERED NURSES (RNs)

Registered nurses care for the mental, physical and emotional needs of sick and injured patients. In hospitals, RNs provide bedside care in a specific area, such as surgery or maternity, where they carry out medical regimens prescribed by physicians. In nursing homes, they care for residents. They assess patients' medical conditions, develop treatments and perform difficult procedures, such as starting intravenous fluids.

In government and private agencies, clinics, schools and retirement communities, RNs teach about nutrition, childcare and home care for the sick and handicapped. They also may administer immunizations and perform routine tests.

**Private-duty nurses** work directly with families, nursing homes or temporary help agencies. **Office nurses** assist physicians in private practice, clinics and surgical centers. **Occupational health or industrial nurses** care for employees with minor injuries and illnesses at work sites. **Head nurses** direct nursing activities, plan work schedules, assign duties and order supplies.

***Required skills/personal attributes.*** Registered nurses should be sympathetic, yet have the emotional stability to cope with suffering, emergencies and other daily stresses. They must be able to follow orders precisely and use good judgment in determining when consultation is needed. Physical stamina is essential. Those with supervisory responsibilities must have leadership qualities.

***Work environment.*** RNs work in well-lighted, comfortable medical facilities. Public health nurses travel in all types of weather to visit homes, schools and community centers. Often, nurses must work nights, weekends and holidays.

***Education/training/certification.*** There are three major educational paths: RNs may earn a two-year associate degree (ADN), a diploma from a two- to three-year hospital-sponsored program or a bachelor of science degree in nursing (BSN) from a four-year college or university.

All states require RNs to be licensed after graduation from an accredited nursing school. Candidates must pass a national exam. Nurses may be licensed in more than one state, either by taking an examination or through reciprocal endorsement. Continuing education is a requirement for license renewal in some states.

***Salary range.*** In 1991, full-time staff nurses in private hospitals earned from $15.17 to $21.82 an hour. Part-time staff nurses earned about $17.14. RNs working in nursing homes earned an average $12.96. Many employers offer flexible work schedules, childcare and educational benefits.

***Opportunities for advancement/career growth.*** Increasingly, management-level positions require a graduate degree. Within patient care, nurses may advance to clinical nurse specialist, nurse midwife or another specialty area with a one- to two-year graduate education leading to certification or a master's degree.

The outlook for RNs is excellent throughout the '90s. Hospitals coping with shortages of qualified nurses have hired support staff to handle routine duties, so that nurses can be more efficient. However, most growth is expected in outpatient facilities in hospitals, offices and clinics, ambulatory surgicenters and emergency medical centers. Jobs in nursing homes and home health care will increase, as an aging population requires long-term care and hospitals release patients earlier.

***Drawbacks for part-timers.*** None.

***Advantages for part-timers.*** About a quarter of RNs work part-time.

***For more information.*** Write to The National League of Nursing (NLN), 350 Hudson St., New York, NY 10014.

# RESERVATION AND TRANSPORTATION TICKET CLERKS

In addition to answering questions and offering suggestions on travel arrangements such as routes, time schedules, rates and types of accommodations, **reservation agents** make and confirm transportation and hotel reservations, calculate expenses and write and sell tickets. They also check baggage and direct passengers to their point of departure.

Reservation agents usually answer phone inquiries and book, change and cancel reservations from central offices. With access to a computer terminal, they can quickly obtain up-to-date information.

**Ticket clerks** compile and record information, such as dates of travel and method of payment. **Ticket agents** sell tickets, answer inquires, check baggage, examine passports and visas, ensure passenger seating and check in animals. Others, commonly known as **gate agents**, take flight tickets, make arrival and departure announcements and assist passengers in boarding airplanes.

**Travel clerks** are employed by automobile clubs to plan trips and offer travel suggestions to club members. Using a road map, they show the best route from the point of origin to the destination. They also may indicate points of interest, restaurants and accommodations enroute and explain available emergency repair services.

***Required skills/personal attributes.*** Reservation and transportation ticket clerks should have a pleasant appearance, personality and speaking voice. They must be knowledgeable about company policies and procedures and aware of special promotions and services. Problem-solving skills and computer literacy are important.

**Work environment.** Seven out of 10 reservation and ticket clerks are employed by major airlines and work in comfortable, well-lighted offices or at large, metropolitan airports. Others work for automobile clubs, hotels and other companies providing transportation services. Much of their work is repetitious. Prolonged exposure to video display terminals may lead to eye and muscle strain.

**Education/training/certification.** Most clerks learn skills in company-sponsored training programs that cover computer usage, telephone etiquette, interpersonal and time-management skills.

**Salary range.** In 1990, full-time reservation and transportation ticket clerks earned about $390 a week. They also receive free or low-cost travel on company carriers for themselves and families.

**Opportunities for advancement/career growth.** Clerks may advance to supervisory positions or become field sales agents. Increased business travel is expected to spur employment growth in the '90s. In addition, more two-income families, as well as smaller families, should have more discretionary income for leisure travel.

**Drawbacks for part-timers.** Competition for jobs will be fierce. The travel and transportation industries are sensitive to cyclical swings in the economy. Night, weekend and holiday shifts are necessary for those who lack seniority.

**Advantages for part-timers.** Schedules and shifts are flexible. Part-time work is common. Even part-timers are often able to qualify for free or low-cost travel.

**For more information.** Write to the Air Line Employees Association, 5600 South Central Ave., Chicago, IL 60638.

# RESPIRATORY THERAPISTS

Respiratory therapists evaluate, treat and care for patients—from premature infants to the elderly—who have breathing disorders. They test the capacity of a patient's lungs, analyze oxygen and carbon dioxide concentrations and measure acidity or alkalinity levels of the blood. The results are presented to physicians.

Therapists may treat patients with chronic asthma, emphysema or victims of heart failure, stroke or shock with oxygen or oxygen mixtures, chest physiotherapy and aerosol medications. Patients who need help removing mucus from their lungs after surgery or who suffer from lung disease or cystic fibrosis, may be treated with chest physiotherapy. Therapists may apply an oxygen mask or connect a patient to a ventilator that delivers pressurized air to the lungs. They keep records and check patients and equipment settings, making changes according to doctors' orders.

In home care, the therapists teach patients and their families how to use mechanical ventilators and other life support systems. They may visit several times a month to inspect the equipment.

***Required skills/personal attributes.*** Respiratory therapists should be sensitive to the physical and psychological needs of patients. Attention to detail, manual dexterity and mechanical ability are important. Therapists also must be able follow instructions, and work as part of a team. Knowledge of mathematics, chemical reactions and physical principles are important.

***Work environment.*** Respiratory therapists spend long periods standing and walking between patients' rooms. In emergency rooms, they work under stress. Pressurized gases are potentially hazardous. They may risk infection from AIDS and other diseases from needle pricks when drawing blood for analysis of blood gases.

***Education/training/certification.*** One-, two-, and four-year training programs are offered in hospitals, medical schools, colleges and universities, trade schools, vocational-technical institutes and the military. The National Board of Respiratory Care awards two credentials to practitioners: Certified Respiratory Therapy Technician (CRTT) at the entry level, and Registered Respiratory Therapist (RRT) for positions in intensive care and management.

***Salary range.*** In 1991, part-time respiratory therapists earned about $13 an hour.

***Opportunities for advancement/career growth.*** Nine out of 10 respiratory therapists work in respiratory care, anesthesiology or pulmonary medicine departments of hospitals. Others work for home health agencies and nursing homes. Experienced respiratory therapists may advance to supervisory or managerial positions.

An aging population will heighten the incidence of cardio-pulmonary disease. Employment opportunities are expected to be good in developing neonatal and cardiopulmonary care specialties. There will also be some growth in home health agencies, equipment and rental companies and firms that provide care on a contractual basis.

***Drawbacks for part-timers.*** Evening and weekend shifts may be necessary in hospitals and nursing homes.

***Advantages for part-timers.*** Part-time work is common and schedules and shifts are flexible, especially in hospitals and home health agencies.

***For more information.*** Write to the American Association of Respiratory Care, 11030 Ables Lane, Dallas, TX 75229.

# RETAIL SALES WORKERS

By describing product features, demonstrating function and showing various models and colors, retail sales workers try to interest consumers in purchasing a wide variety of goods. Those who sell expensive items, such as cars or computers, need special knowledge of various brands and models and the meaning of manufacturer's specifications.

When they make a sale, most retail sales workers fill out sales checks, receive cash, checks or charge payments and bag purchases or arrange for mailing or delivery. Those who use a cash register may be responsible for counting money, separating change from charge slips, coupons and exchange vouchers and making deposits at the cash office.

Sales workers also handle returns and exchanges, stock shelves, mark price tags, take inventory and prepare displays. They must be aware of store promotions, as well as policies and procedures, and be able to recognize and handle security risks.

***Required skills/personal attributes.*** Retail sales workers should be courteous, efficient and enjoy serving customers. They should have patience and tact and be able to listen and communicate clearly. Some employers may conduct a background check before hiring sales workers, especially those who sell expensive items.

***Work environment.*** Most salespeople in the retail trade work in clean, well-lighted stores. They stand for long periods and may need supervisory approval to leave the sales floor.

***Education/training/certification.*** Many people get their first jobs in retail sales. In smaller stores, on-the-job training is informal. In larger stores, training programs are more formal and usually conducted over several days. Specialized training also may be provided by a manufacturer's representative.

***Salary range.*** Compensation systems vary by the type of establishment and merchandise sold. Most are paid a small salary with the opportunity to earn commissions on sales. Benefits tend to be few in small stores, but nearly all salespeople are able to buy their store's merchandise at a discount of up to 40 percent. In some cases, this discount also may be extended to family members. Starting pay for many part-time positions is minimum wage.

***Opportunities for advancement/career growth.*** With experience and seniority, retail salespeople take on additional responsibility. In small stores, sales workers can become assistant managers. A college education is becoming increasingly important for management jobs, but capable people without a degree can advance to administrative and supervisory work in large stores.

Retail sales experience can be an asset when applying for sales positions with larger retailers and in other industries. In the '90s, increased competition will prompt many department stores to add more workers in an effort to improve customer service.

***Drawbacks for part-timers.*** Evening and weekend work is common and longer-than-normal hours may be scheduled during Christmas and other peak periods. Sometimes schedules are set weekly, making planning difficult. During recessions, managers often cut staff. Turnover tends to be high. Part-timers are rarely hired to sell expensive items, such as cars, furniture and electronic equipment, for which the earnings are the best.

***Advantages for part-timers.*** There continue to be an abundance of opportunities for part-time and temporary workers who can fill in during peak selling periods. Because more stores keep long hours, the opportunity to negotiate flexible schedules is good. In many stores, "full-time" is less than 40 hours a week. Some retail workers are self-employed representatives of direct sales companies and mail-order houses and can set their own schedules. Some stores employ personal shoppers, part-time or by appointment, to assist customers in purchasing gift items or updating their wardrobes.

***For more information.*** Write to the National Retail Federation, 100 West 31st St., New York, NY 10001.

# SERVICE SALES REPRESENTATIVES

Service sales representatives sell a variety of services in industries as diverse as education, data processing, hotel/convention, fund raising, temporary help services and telecommunications.

Using telephone and business directories that cover their assigned territories, as well as leads from business associates and customers, they identify prospective clients and contact them. They may send printed information about the services they sell or visit prospects to demonstrate services in face-to-face meetings.

Sales representatives must become thoroughly familiar with their prospects' business operations. They often work as part of a team to compile technical proposals that answer client needs. Some sales representatives deal with several prospective clients. Others have one client with many ongoing needs.

***Required skills/personal attributes.*** Service sales representatives should be highly motivated, well-organized and efficient.

They should be self-starters with the ability to work under pressure to meet sales goals. Self-confidence, reliability and the ability to communicate well—orally and in writing—are important. A pleasant personality and neat appearance are helpful.

**Work environment.** Many service sales representatives spend a great deal of time—sometimes weeks—traveling a territory. Those with a relatively small territory spend time preparing various documents and setting appointments with customers. Those who sell exclusively by telephone work in an office.

Competition from other companies, as well as from fellow sales representatives competing for company-established goals or sales quotas, can be stressful. Computer literacy is a plus for improving productivity.

**Education/training/certification.** Many employers require a college degree in business, marketing or a field related to the service offered. Many large companies also conduct intensive formal training programs to teach new representatives about company services and sales techniques. Frequent follow-up training sessions update representatives on new products or services and help them maintain and update sales skills.

**Salary range.** In 1990, the average salary for full-time service sales representatives was $24,400 to $26,000. However, successful sales representatives can often earn more than $100,000 a year. Sales representatives who handle technical services tend to earn more than nontechnical reps.

Some representatives earn a straight salary. Others earn only commissions. Most earn a combination of salary and commission.

Many have the use of a company car and an expense account to cover travel and entertaining. They also have numerous opportunities to earn incentive bonuses, such as vacation trips, for exceeding their sales quota.

**Opportunities for advancement/career growth.** Large companies prefer to hire college graduates. Smaller companies often hire those with proven sales experience. Service sales representatives with good sales records and leadership ability may advance to sales supervisors and then branch or district managers. Some go into business as independent representatives.

The growth of sales jobs is directly related to the growth of service industries. Health care and personal services are industries to watch in the '90s.

*Drawbacks for part-timers.* Turnover is high for sales representatives who handle nontechnical services. Earnings for all reps may fluctuate with changing economic conditions and shifting consumer preferences.

*Advantages for part-timers.* Many reps have the flexibility to set their own schedules, as long as they meet company goals.

*For more information.* Contact employers who sell services in your area.

# SOCIAL WORKERS

Social workers help individuals and families cope with problems such as homelessness, unemployment, financial mismanagement, serious illness, substance abuse, unwanted pregnancy and divorce.

They often provide practical information, such as where to go for debt counseling, how to find childcare or eldercare and how to be admitted to a rehabilitation program. They may pull together a number of services, and then follow through to assure that services are provided.

Most social workers specialize in a particular area. **Child welfare workers** counsel children and young people and help find foster homes for neglected and abandoned children. Those in **child or adult protective services** investigate reports of abuse and neglect and may institute legal action. **Mental health social workers** may conduct group therapy, crisis intervention and training for the mentally disabled. **Medical social workers** help patients and families cope with chronic terminal illnesses and organize support groups for families of patients. **School social workers** counsel problem and handicapped students, and arrange for needed services. **Criminal justice social workers** may make recommendations to courts and conduct pre-sentencing assessments. **Industrial social workers** offer counseling to employees affected by emotional or family problems or substance abuse. **Clinical or psychiatric social workers** provide psychotherapy. Some specialize in gerontological services and run support groups for family caregivers or adult children of aging parents.

*Required skills/personal attributes.* Social workers should be emotionally stable, objective and sensitive. They must be able to handle responsibility and work independently. Interpersonal skills are essential.

*Work environment.* Although they spend most of their working hours in offices or residential facilities, social workers also may travel to visit clients or meet with service providers. The work can be emotionally draining and stressful because of chronic understaffing. Most social workers are employed in urban areas.

*Education/training/certification.* A bachelor's degree in social work (BSW), psychology, sociology or a related field is the minimum requirement for direct service positions, such as caseworker. A master's degree in social work (MSW) is generally necessary for positions in health and mental health settings and public agencies.

In 1990, almost all states had licensing, certification or registration laws regarding the practice of social work and the use of professional titles. Voluntary certification is offered by the National Association of Social Workers (NASW), which grants the titles Academy of Certified Social Workers (ACSW) or Academy of Certified Baccalaureate Social Workers (ACBSW)) to those who qualify. For clinical social workers, especially those in private practice, professional credentials include listing in the NASW Register of Clinical Social Workers or the Directory of American Board of Examiners in Clinical Social Work.

*Salary range.* In 1991, full-time medical social workers in private hospitals earned $14.73 an hour. In 1990, social workers in all types of settings earned from $23,000 to $36,000 per year.

*Opportunities for advancement/career growth.* Advancement in social work usually requires an MSW degree. Employment in hospitals and private social security agencies is expected to grow much faster than average in the '90s. For the same reason, opportunities in home health care also will open up in the years ahead.

Some social workers with MSW degrees go into private practice as clinical social workers. Opportunities in private practice are expected to increase because of the anticipated availability of funding from health insurance and public sector contracts. In addition, the growing popularity of employee assistance programs among corporations is expected to spur demand for private practitioners.

Other career options for social workers are teaching, research and consulting.

***Drawbacks for part-timers.*** Chronic understaffing may make it difficult to negotiate part-time hours. Some social workers must be available nights and weekends and on call to cope with emergencies.

***Advantages for part-timers.*** Part-time work can be found in voluntary nonprofit agencies. Consultants, teachers and those is private practice have more flexibility in setting their own hours.

***For more information.*** Write to the National Association of Social Workers, 7981 Eastern Ave., Silver Spring, MD 20910.

# SPEECH-LANGUAGE PATHOLOGISTS AND AUDIOLOGISTS

**Speech-language pathologists** assess and treat people with speech, language, voice and fluency disorders, such as stuttering. They may work with people who can't make speech sounds, understand or produce language, have motor problems that make it difficult to eat and swallow or suffer from impairment caused by an injury, stroke or birth defect.

Using special instruments as well as oral and written tests, pathologists analyze irregularities. They may select alternative communication systems, such as automated devices or sign language, for those with little or no speech.

**Audiologists** assess and treat people with hearing disorders. Using audiometers and other testing devices they measure the loudness at which people hear certain sounds and assess their ability to distinguish between sounds. Audiologists may examine and clean a patient's ear canal, fit hearing aids and train patients in lip reading.

Speech-language pathologists and audiologists may work independently or as part of a team in speech, language and hearing clinics. Each keeps records and counsels patients and their families.

*Required skills/personal attributes.* Speech-language pathologists and audiologists should be patient, compassionate and able to effectively communicate test results, diagnoses and proposed treatments in a manner easily understood by patients. Attention to detail and concentration are essential.

*Work environment.* Pathologists and audiologists spend most of their time at desks in clean, comfortable surroundings. Those who work on a contract may spend a substantial amount of time traveling between facilities.

*Education/training/certification.* Of the 40 states that license audiologists and 39 that license speech-language pathologists, all require a master's degree or equivalent.

With a master's degree, a pathologist or audiologist can acquire the Certificate of Clinical Competence (CCC) offered by the American Speech-Language-Hearing Association. Applicants must have 300 hours of clinical experience and have completed a nine-month post-graduate internship.

*Salary range.* In 1990, full-time speech-language pathologists with up to three years of experience earned from $25,000 to $38,000. Full-time audiologists earned from $26,000 to $42,000.

*Opportunities for advancement/career growth.* About half of all speech-language pathologists and audiologists provide services in schools. About 10 percent are in hospitals. Others work in physicians' offices, speech, language and learning centers, home health care agencies and other facilities. Some are in private practice, working solo or as part of a group. Some provide contract or consulting services. Others design and develop equipment or conduct research. Employment opportunities are expected to increase faster than average for both pathologists and audiologists.

***Drawbacks for part-timers.*** None.

***Advantages for part-timers.*** The number of pathologists and audiologists in private practice is expected to rise sharply by the year 2005. Hospitals, schools and nursing homes are expected to increase their use of contract services, and new legislation for children with disabilities may extend care to children from 3 to 5 years old.

***For more information.*** Write to the American Speech-Language-Hearing Association, 10801 Rockville Pike, Rockville, MD 20852.

# SURGICAL TECHNOLOGISTS

Surgical technologists assist in operations under the supervision of surgeons or registered nurses. They help set up the operating room with surgical instruments and other materials. They also may "prep" patients for surgery.

After transporting patients to the operating room and covering them with special surgical drapes, technologists pass instruments and other sterile supplies to surgeons and assistants during the operation. They may assist in other ways, such as caring for and diagnosing specimens taken for laboratory analysis and helping to operate diagnostic equipment. After the operation, surgical technologists transport patients to recovery rooms and clean and restock the operating room.

***Required skills/personal attributes.*** Surgical technologists need physical stamina. They must be emotionally stable and able to concentrate throughout an operation that may last several hours. In addition to organization and knowledge of surgical procedures, technologists should have excellent manual dexterity and be able to respond quickly to a surgeon's instructions.

**Work environment.** Surgical technologists work in clean, well-lighted, cool operating rooms. Most surgery is performed during the day. But in some workplaces, such as emergency surgical units, surgical technologists may be on call to work evenings and weekends on a rotating basis.

**Education/training/certification.** Formal programs, combining classroom study and clinical supervision, are offered by community and junior colleges, vocational-technical institutes and hospitals. One- or two-year programs lead to a certificate or associate degree. Hospital programs last from six months to a year. Shorter programs are available for licensed practical nurses who already have some medical experience. Some surgical technologists are trained by the military. All are expected to stay up-to-date on new developments in the field.

Idaho is the only state that requires surgical technologists to be licensed. But many employers prefer to hire technologists who've been awarded voluntary certification from the Liaison Council on Certification. Candidates must have graduated from a formal training program and pass a written examination. Continuing education or re-examination is required to renew certification every six years.

**Salary range.** In 1991, surgical technologists earned from $9.46 to $13.03 an hour.

**Opportunities for advancement/career growth.** Most surgical technologists are employed by hospitals. Others work in physicians' offices and clinics. A few, known as "private scrubs," are employed directly by surgeons who have special teams, such as those for liver transplants.

Career advancement is limited. Some technologists may advance to first assistants. With additional training, they can work with lasers and assist in more complex procedures, such as open-heart surgery. Some take positions with insurance companies or sterile supply services, or become instructors in surgical technology programs.

Employment opportunities for surgical technologists look bright as the volume of surgery increases and operating-room staff patterns change. Some employers prefer to use surgical technologists rather then operating room nurses to cut costs.

Technologists will find more opportunities outside of hospitals as more procedures are performed at a growing number of outpatient offices, clinics and ambulatory surgicenters.

***Drawbacks for part-timers.*** Many technologists working in hospitals are on call in the evening and during weekends.

***Advantages for part-timers.*** Those who work in offices and clinics where most surgery is scheduled may have more control over work hours and can negotiate flexible arrangements.

***For more information.*** Write to the Association of Surgical Technologists, 7108-C S. Alton Way, Englewood, CO 80112.

# TEACHER AIDES

Teacher aides help supervise students in the classroom, in the cafeteria and on field trips. In addition to recording grades, setting up equipment and helping prepare materials for instruction, they may tutor children. Some teacher aides handle only routine, clerical tasks such as grading tests and papers, checking homework, keeping attendance records, typing, filing and duplicating materials.

Others instruct children under the direction and guidance of a teacher. They may work with children individually or in small groups to review classwork and help find information for reports. Some coordinate special projects, such as science demonstrations.

***Required skills/personal attributes.*** Teacher aides should enjoy working with children. They should be patient and fair and willingly follow a teacher's direction. Good oral and writing skills and interpersonal relations are important. Clerical skills, a familiarity with audiovisual equipment and instructional materials may also be necessary.

***Work environment.*** Teacher aides work in the classroom and outdoors. They spend a lot of time standing, walking and kneeling. The work can be physically and emotionally draining.

***Education/training/certification.*** Requirements range from a high school diploma to some college training for aides with teaching responsibilities. A number of two-year and community colleges offer associate degree programs. Most employers prefer to hire aides who have experience working with children.

***Salary range.*** In 1990, teacher aides earned about $7.50 per hour. Many are covered by collective bargaining agreements and have benefits.

***Opportunities for advancement/career growth.*** Advancement, usually in the form of higher earnings or increased responsibility, comes with experience and additional education. Some school districts allow aides time away from the job to attend additional college courses. With a bachelor's degree, a teacher aide may become a certified teacher. Employment opportunities, especially in special education, are expected to grow dramatically throughout the '90s.

***Drawbacks for part-timers.*** Government spending cuts for education will affect employment of teacher aides. Pay is low and advancement is limited.

***Advantages for part-timers.*** About half of all teacher aides work part-time during the traditional school year.

***For more information.*** Write to the American Federation of Teachers, Organizing Department, 555 New Jersey Ave. NW, Washington, DC 20001.

# TRAVEL AGENTS

Depending on needs of their individual clients, travel agents may suggest destinations, make arrangements for transportation, hotel accommodations, car rentals, tours and recreation for a vacation package or business/pleasure trip.

They may advise travelers about weather conditions, restaurants and attractions. For international travelers, they provide information on customs regulations, required papers (passports, visas, certificates of vaccination) and currency exchange rates.

To stay up-to-date on a range of destinations, travel agents consult a wide variety of published and computer-based sources for information on departure and arrival times, rates, hotel ratings and activities. They have many opportunities to visit hotels, resorts and restaurants in a variety of locations so they can base recommendations on their personal experience.

***Required skills/personal attributes.*** In addition to travel experience, agents should be pleasant, patient and able to gain the confidence of clients and motivate them to travel.

***Work environment.*** Travel agents spend most of their time in comfortable, well-lighted offices. Throughout the day they confer with clients, complete paperwork and use the telephone and computer to contact airlines, hotels and other sources. During peak holidays and vacation seasons, they may work under a great deal of pressure.

***Education/training/certification.*** Specialized training is becoming increasingly important because fewer agencies are willing to train agents on the job. Many vocational schools offer three- to 12-week, full-time programs, as well as Saturday and evening classes. Training is also offered in public adult education programs and community and four-year colleges. A few colleges offers bachelor's and master's degree in travel and tourism. Courses in business, computer skills, languages and geography are useful.

Several home study programs provide a basic understanding of the travel industry. The American Society of Travel Agents (ASTA) and the Institute of Certified Travel Agents both offer a travel correspondence courses.

Experienced travel agents can take an 18-month-long course leading to the designation of Certified Travel Counselor offered by the Institute of Certified Travel Agents. Another recognized mark of achievement is a certificate of proficiency from ASTA, awarded to those who pass a three-hour-long examination.

There is no federal licensing requirement for travel agents. However, two states require certification and three states require registration.

*Salary range.* In 1990, full-time travel agents with less than a year of experience earned about $12,056. Those with 10 or more years earned $21,715. Those who run their own agencies depend on commissions from airlines (about 10 to 11 percent of a total sale). Travel agents often travel free or at substantially reduced rates.

*Opportunities for advancement/career growth.* In franchise agencies or agencies with many offices, travel agents may advance to office manager. Experienced agents can start their own agency.

As business activity expands to international markets, more businesspeople, professionals and sales representatives will be traveling widely. Rising incomes as well as competition among airlines will encourage more people to plan vacations.

*Drawbacks for part-timers.* Many travel agents work long hours. The industry is extremely sensitive to economic downturns.

*Advantages for part-timers.* Self-employed travel agents may have more flexibility in setting their own hours.

*For more information.* Write to the American Society of Travel Agents, 1101 King St., Alexandria, VA 22314.

# WRITERS AND EDITORS

Writers create original fiction and nonfiction for books, magazines, trade journals, newspapers, technical journals, company newsletters, radio and television broadcasts and advertisements. With an assignment or topic, writers gather information through personal observation, library research and interviews.

**Newswriters** write informative stories for newspapers and news broadcasts, based on information supplied by reporters or wire services. **Columnists** analyze news and write commentaries based on their personal viewpoint. **Editorial writers** stimulate or mold public opinion in accordance with their publication's viewpoint. **Technical writers** put scientific and technical information into readily understandable language. **Copywriters** write advertisements to promote the sale of goods and services in publications or broadcast media.

Many established writers work on a freelance basis, selling their work to publishers, manufacturing firms, public relations and advertising departments or agencies. Some are hired to complete specific assignments, such as writing about a new product or service.

**Editors** supervise writers and may write, rewrite and edit the content of books, magazines or newspapers. Editors may also oversee production.

In small organizations, a single editor often has full responsibility for an entire publication. In larger firms, an executive editor oversees associate or assistant editors who have responsibility for particular subjects such as fiction, reports and sports. Editors hire writers and other employees, plan budgets and negotiate contracts with freelance writers.

*Required skills/personal attributes.* Writers must be able to express a wide range of ideas clearly and concisely. Both writers and editors should be creative, intellectually curious and self-motivated. Attention to detail and perseverance are essential, as is good judgment. Interpersonal skills are important. Most writers and editors should be familiar with personal computers, word processors and electronic desktop publishing systems.

*Work environment.* Conditions vary with the firm and type of publication. Some writers and editors work in comfortable, private offices. Others work in noisy newsrooms, filled with the sounds of keyboards, computer printers and voices. Travel to interview clients or conduct research is common. Many writers and editors spend a great deal of time on the telephone. Pressure to produce under strict deadline can be stressful.

*Education/training/certification.* Employers prefer writers who have a broad liberal arts background and a bachelor's degree in communications, journalism or English. Technical writers should have a degree in a specialized field and/or some practical knowledge.

*Salary range.* In 1990, beginning writers earned about $20,000 a year. With five years of experience, they earned about $30,000.

Technical writers and editors working in the federal government earned an average $36,897. Senior editors at large newspapers earned more than $60,000.

***Opportunities for advancement/career growth.*** Practical experience is invaluable, beginning with work on a high school or college newspaper.

Our obsession with information will continue to open up many opportunities for writers and editors throughout the '90s. As technology advances, there also will be a growing demand for technical writers. Those who work for computer software firms or manufacturers are typically concentrated in the Northeast, Texas and California. Writers who work for major book publishers, magazines, broadcasting companies, advertising agencies and public relations firms and the federal government are concentrated in large metropolitan areas. Advertising and public relations will be strong areas, but competitive.

***Drawbacks for part-timers.*** Most full-time writers and editors work a traditional work week—and put in longer hours close to the deadline for publication. Night and weekend work is required for those who prepare morning or weekend publications and broadcasts.

***Advantages for part-timers.*** Many writers work as freelancers. Although they may work evening and weekend hours to meet a deadline, they have greater control over their schedules and the projects they accept.

***For more information.*** Write to the Dow Jones Newspaper Fund, P.O. Box 300, Princeton, NJ 08540.

# Part 3

# New ways to work: Finding nontraditional career options in the corporate world

*"Men, for the sake of getting a living, forget to live."*
—Margaret Fuller

# Chapter 7

# Part-time corporate: Redefining 9-to-5

What's so sacred about 9-to-5? For an increasing number of professionals—mostly women with preschool-age children—9-to-5 means rushing around in the morning and always being worn out at dinner time. It means arriving home too late to meet your daughter's school bus or catch the start of your son's soccer game. Worst of all, it means ceding too many smiles and first words and precious moments to the latest day-care provider.

Yet, if you can afford to work part-time—are you willing to risk derailing the career you worked so hard to build on a "mommy track"?

Whoever said you can "have it all" had it all wrong.

While young mothers are not the only people asking for part-time and flexible work arrangements, as the fastest-growing segment of the work force, they are driving significant change. From 1978 to 1988, the number of working mothers with children under the age of 3 leapt from just over 39 percent of the labor force in 1978 to 52.5 percent in 1988. A group with this kind of clout is impossible to ignore. So it should come as little surprise that the issues of single parents and two-income families have landed squarely on corporate agendas.

Meanwhile, there are a few other things on the corporate agenda. The spiraling cost of doing business has executives greedily eyeing payrolls—laden with rich benefits and overhead expenses—for cut-backs.

Two agendas on a collision course? Yes, and no. We've already felt the impact of dramatic changes in the traditionally rock-solid corporate world. And it's not over yet. Throughout the '90s, companies will continue to restructure staffing and streamline operations to remain competitive. It is not only possible, but probable, that we have seen the last of the world of work as we have known it throughout most of this decade.

In a new world-in-flux, every "standard" is likely to be up for grabs. Therein lies the opportunity for professionals interested in more flexibility—because flexibility will be the byword in the coming decade. Companies need flexible options for staffing. Parents need flexible work arrangements. Companies need to retain the expertise of seasoned professionals. Parents need more elastic hours to care for children. Rather than continuing to play the roles of parent and child, companies and employees can both profit by becoming partners.

Let's take a closer look at the dynamics at work in the world of work.

## The work force is changing

Professional women who delayed childbearing in the '70s and '80s are starting to have families in the '90s—and waking up to the realities of the other full-time job they've taken on.

Holly Angus scaled her hours as production manager down to three days a week so she could spend more unstructured time with her 3-year-old son Teddy. "I got the feeling that he needed more from his parents as the people he looks to for discipline on a steady, no-big-deal basis. It's hard when you come home tired and cranky and you have to make dinner and do laundry," she says. Although it has meant less money for frills, as well as less satisfying work as "floater" in her department, for the time being it is well worth it.

These days, instead of negotiating with printers at 10 on a Wednesday morning, she's playing Candyland with her son. "There's no deadline, no timetable. I don't have to jump up and do the laundry. I can just be with him and not feel like I should be doing anything instead of playing Candyland."

There is evidence that more fathers are concerned about balancing family obligations with career progress. When the Du Pont Company surveyed its 6,600 employees in 1988, 25 percent of the males responding were interested in having more flexible scheduling to meet family and personal needs. The 1991 survey showed 35 percent of the men were for more time off.

While only a small percentage of men in the company are actually taking advantage of the flexibility, Du Pont's example seems to indicate that we are plodding in the right direction.

The most liberal Family and Medical Leave Act in the country's history now guarantees both men and women working in companies with more than 50 employees 12 weeks of unpaid leave for birth or adoption or other family obligations. It is long overdue, but still a small step. Even it were financially feasible for both parents to take the maximum leave, many men remain reluctant to buck the unwritten ethic that says: "If you're serious, you're here."

Some men find flexibility in smaller firms or less-structured industries. "There's a real awareness here," says Scott Johnson, one of three partners in the Dean Johnson Design firm in Indianapolis. "I'm a single parent and have my children every other week. On 'kid-week,' I have to be out of here by 5:30—no if's, and's or but's. If we're busy, I may have to take things home with me or work out a way to get a project done with someone else's help. On the weeks when I don't have my kids with me I can stay as late as I need to."

Quality childcare is essential to working families. But it is still difficult to find and keep affordable arrangements. And what about those hours after school? Holidays? Sick days? Summer vacation?

When her son came down with chicken pox, followed a week later by her twins, Beverly Dinan was in a bind. Fortunately, she and her husband were able to share sick-duty. "I'd come home for the morning. He'd come home for the afternoon. He's a supervisor (both work at Aetna Life & Casualty Co.), so he has less flexibility, which makes it a little tougher," she admits.

## Business is changing

Even a decade ago, landing a good job with a solid company meant you were "in." All you had to worry about was moving up. Changing demographics and a fiercely competitive marketplace have conspired to change all that.

Just to remain in the game, large and small companies must trim down and shape up their performance, making payroll a prime target. As a result, many of us are worried about being moved out before we have a chance to move up. Layoffs in the tens of thousands of employees continue to shake the foundations of traditionally solid corporations, such as IBM. The number of full-time employees in Fortune 500 companies has been sliced nearly in half over the last two decades. Even the term "permanent" is not spoken in the same breath as "employee" at many companies.

Nothing is permanent. Long-term commitments are no longer possible.

If you're planning to sit tight and wait for better times to return, you may have a long wait. Companies are cautiously restructuring operations around a "core" of employees best suited to carry out their primary business. That means more tasks will be to doled out to part-timers and just-in-time workers, such as temporaries or contractors.

## The good news for part-time professionals

Already, fully one-third of all American workers work part-time, or have temporary or contract jobs. More than 90 percent of the 365,000 jobs created by U.S. companies early in 1993 were part-time positions. By the end of the decade, this work force is expected to outnumber full-time workers.

A number of factors will determine who in this group will be positioned to thrive in the years ahead.

The labor force—at high tide during the '70s—will hit a low ebb in the '90s. According to *Workforce 2000* published by the Indianapolis-based Hudson Institute, we can expect the labor force to grow only 1 percent per year instead of the robust 2.9 percent per year of two decades ago, reflecting a dramatic drop in the birth rate.

Smart companies will work hard to protect their most valuable assets—trained, skilled employees. Some analysts place the cost of replacing a skilled professional as high as one and a half times the employee's annual salary. Faced with losing the expertise of proven professionals to maternity leave, more companies are open to more flexible schedules to accommodate the needs of new mothers. When they must recruit new talent, this new generation of "family-friendly" companies uses flexible policies to court the best and brightest.

**The Corning solution.** In the mid 1980s, Corning noticed that women were leaving the company at twice the rate of white males. So in 1987 the New York State-based firm, which competes in the fields of laboratory sciences, telecommunications and specialty materials, launched a policy encouraging part-time work options, including job-sharing and work-from-home, for salaried employees. This was no empty gesture. Part-timers are considered for promotion and allowed to have supervisory responsibilities. The company has documented the fact that more high-potential women are staying with the company.

**Productivity: A new attitude.** Most employees cannot afford to work less than full-time. But those who are interested in doing so will tell you that productivity is more likely to flourish in an afternoon free from worry about a fourth-grader's unfinished homework, a day spent at home working without interruptions—or even as part of a team sharing the tasks of one job by blending professional competencies.

Smart companies are beginning to see that results do not always correlate with time-sheet tallies. Often, for example:

- **Service is enhanced by increased coverage.** Job-sharing teams can cover for each other during vacations and provide more effective service to clients. A customer-service staff working flexible hours can stagger schedules to provide just the right amount of coverage—covering a longer period of the day with overlapping hours during peak hours.

- **More heads can reduce the bottom line.** When people work off-site or in less-expensive satellite centers, the cost of overhead is reduced. Salary and benefits are also lower.

- **Goodwill has value.** Employees consider flexibility a privilege well-worth protecting. People working less than full-time say they work smarter. They spend less time in casual conversation at the water cooler. And because they feel less stress over family obligations, they report to work fresher, with more energy for work. The positive effect of intangibles, such as better morale and increased loyalty, may be difficult to measure—but impossible to ignore.

**The U S West way.** At this Denver-based Baby Bell, telecommuting is widespread. Public relations manager Cathy Fowler says the company's liberal policy has proven to be a powerful productivity tool. "Employees appreciate it so much that they are willing to put forth the effort to make it work. It's considered a perk. Therefore, employees want to make sure that their bosses are getting their money's worth." If someone happens to slack off, she says, peers notice and take action. "They'll say, 'Look, we worked hard for this. Don't mess it up for us.'"

## The new partnership: Finding common ground

At Levi Strauss & Co., about 100 employees are taking an active role in helping the company streamline its operations—a task that conceivably could eliminate their own jobs.

According to Helen Purdum, pension benefits specialist, full-time employees volunteered to leave their regular jobs and departments to go to work on one of about a dozen task forces. Over the course of six months, these groups will interview employees in every department throughout the company. This is a serious and painstaking process according to Helen. "They're looking at every single operation and charting the work flow. We have a chance to correct them when they've heard us wrong."

In light of the fact that there are sure to be changes company-wide as a result of task force findings, Helen thinks the company's open and above-board attitude can only help employees deal with a "nervous" situation. Employees are invited to open houses held on the floor currently occupied by members of the task force—and they read about the group's progress in a special newsletter. At regular company-wide meetings, chief executive officer Bob Haas provides an executive-level overview.

A veteran of the front line during plant closings in the '80s, Helen is pleased with Levi Strauss's straightforward and "down-to-earth" approach to employee communication. The message is: "The job is not a given. Changes are allowed, so just don't get too attached to your job." Consequently, she says "People know they won't be in the same chair for 30 years."

## The employee as partner

Even if your company isn't saying it in so many words, you should begin to think of yourself less as an employee and more as an entrepreneur. To succeed in having a satisfying career in the years ahead, you will have to be resourceful enough to build and maintain new competencies and assertive enough to sell your skills.

"Even in the context of the organization, you need to be flexible," says Helen. "People are realizing that if they don't become flexible, they're going to be put in a slot that could easily be sliced right out. You need to make sure that nobody hears you say 'I can't do that.' Just say 'Well, that's new to me.' Then find somebody who can help you. I think we need to evolve a different version of mentoring—helping employees learn new tasks and not be so fearful of change."

Some companies have already taken steps to meet employees halfway. Anticipating more changes in the decade ahead, high-tech leader Sun Microsystems opened the doors to its own Career Development Center to help Silicon Valley employees manage the transition.

The company that resists flexibility and turns a deaf ear to the needs of its employees will travel a rough road through the '90s.

An increasing number of companies are surveying employees and answering their requests for more flexibility by putting broad-based work/family policies on the books. Some are very rich and innovative. Others may be little more than lip-service. The continued presence of women—working mothers—in the '90s will keep family issues high on the corporate agenda, especially in companies employing a large number of women.

## The new work/family agenda

"Work/family" is an umbrella term for a wide range of programs and policies designed to help people balance home and work. These can include options for extending the length of the standard 12-week parental leave, offering employees a menu of flexible work arrangements and allowing paid time off for parents who must care for sick children. Flexible work arrangements and alternative scheduling often fall under this umbrella. Some companies, such as Aetna Life & Casualty Co., have hired full-time consultants on family issues to facilitate negotiations for flexible jobs.

Still, the existence of flexible work arrangements for exempt employees is a relatively new phenomenon.

In a survey of 7,500 companies conducted by The Families and Work Institute, a nonprofit research and consulting firm, 86 percent had plans to develop some kind of work/family program.

A closer look at 188 large corporations in 1991 ("Corporate Reference Guide to Work-Family Programs," 1991, The Families and Work Institute) revealed that part-time work remains the most popular option, offered by nearly 88 percent of the companies surveyed. Flextime is on it heels, offered by just over 77 percent of the companies. Job-sharing and telecommuting trailed further behind, offered by fewer than half the companies responding.

In a 1989 study, researchers for Catalyst, a national organization focused on women's career issues, were interested in what kinds of employees were using flexible work arrangements and how well the arrangements were working out in 50 companies, ranging in size from a major corporation with close to 400,000 employees to a 300-person subsidiary of a large telecommunications group.

Supervisors, co-workers, subordinates, even clients reported employees working in flexible arrangements were:

- More productive (65 percent)
- Happier (70 percent)
- Taking shorter maternity leaves (More than 50 percent of women responding said they took a shorter maternity leave than they would have if they had returned full-time.)
- Staying on the job (More than a third of the women responding said they could not or would not have returned to their positions if it were not possible to work a flexible schedule.)

## Customizing the culture: A new management style

Even the most generous written policy will wither in an atmosphere that rewards "macho" employees sweating out 50, 60 or 70 hours a week. Because many flexible work arrangements are approved one-on-one between employee and manager, success depends on a culture that encourages managers to experiment with flexibility.

"Part of our mission in Work/Family Strategies for Aetna is to help managers understand how workplace flexibility can meet both their business needs and the employees' needs," says Michelle Carpenter. "We work directly with human resource people in the different strategic business units, as well as with managers and employees."

# Part-Time Careers

At Bausch & Lomb, the international health care and optics company, a request for flexibility can't be denied unless it has been "thoroughly reviewed" by the human resources department. In other words, a supervisor does not have the power to summarily reject a request for shorter hours or revised starting and quitting times.

At U S West, flexibility is slowly becoming a way of life. "We do have people who have a need for high control," admits Cathy Fowler. "But the ones who are flexible definitely receive dividends. As a corporation, we have to be more flexible in order to be nimble enough to adjust to changes in competition and technology in every facet of the business. This is just another facet."

# Chapter 8

# Part-time corporate: Know your options

"I don't see why anybody would want to work full-time," laughs Beverly Dinan, a variable pay consultant for Aetna Life & Casualty Co. Since the birth of her first child 10 years ago, she has designed a variety of part-time schedules that have allowed her to fit her work life around the needs of her family.

Motherhood can be an unpredictable profession. Very often, the *little* things can make a big difference. "I have the flexibility to call my hours as need be," says Meg Campbell. So when her 9-year-old son needed some assistance with his bus schedule early in the school year, she didn't have to think twice about staying with him until the bus picked him up, then leaving for work later.

Telecommuting is another logical outgrowth of Meg's flexibility. "Tomorrow, I'm going to be working at home on a major presentation. If I stay away from office interruptions, I can make better use of my time," she says.

Every spring, the Laguna Salada School District in northern California hosts a special kind of matchmaking meeting—designed to bring teachers interested in job-sharing together.

# Part-Time Careers

"We're very clear that we don't take any responsibility for matching up partners," says John Perry, director of personnel. "But we do try to facilitate people getting together." With good reason. "When you have two people splitting a job 50-50, you generally end up with about 150 percent," he says.

Three stories. Three very different ways of working around the traditional 9-to-5 day. Let's take a closer look at three of the most common flexible arrangements alive and well in a growing number of companies across the country: part-time work, telecommuting and job-sharing.

## Part-time work: Less is more

Maybe you need just one extra day a week to handle your responsibilities as a new mother. Or you'd like to mold your daily schedule to the arrival of the school bus. Maybe you need a few hours off here and there for yourself—to pursue a personal interest. A part-time schedule can allow you the flexibility you need. As you'll see, part-time schedules can take a variety of shapes.

**Shift-ing hours.** Ten years ago, Beverly Dinan was still breaking ground at Aetna. When her son was born, she moved to a three-day work week. But when she gave birth to twins a year and a half later she opted to add a day to her work week. "All along I'd been saying that when my second child was born, I wanted to stay home," she remembers. "But when the second child was *twins*, it was really too much for one person to handle. I wanted to be in a position where I *wanted* to be with them and not be totally run down by them."

After a year of this, she bought herself an extra day every two weeks by working seven out of every 10 days (with every Friday and every other Monday off). When a project came along she wanted, she moved back to a four-day week. Last March, it was time to change again.

"My son was in fourth-grade and his homework assignments required more of his attention. I wanted to make sure he had a quiet spot," she says. By working five shorter days a week, she can be home within 10 minutes of the school bus in the afternoon. "We can have a snack and then start the homework, so it's pretty much wrapped up by dinner time," she says. When summer comes, she'll go back to four days a week.

Without this kind of flexibility, Beverly would probably not have been able to continue working. "I hear from a lot of people who never even ask. They assume the answer will be no," she says. "My advice would be: Go ahead and push for a trial period. I really think that the climates are loosening up and businesses are recognizing that this could be a very good retention tool."

**Time to explore.** It took some hard times—a divorce, the death of both parents and then a layoff—to convince Madeleine DeCarlo she was ready for a break from 13 years of full-time retail sales. She took six months off. When she went back to work, she started at 28 hours a week behind the Origins (Estee Lauder) cosmetics counter at Macy's. When her hours jumped to the present 33 hours a week, she dropped her other part-time job and realized she had stumbled upon "a blessing."

"I won't give up medical benefits," she insists. "I'm trying to be stable and safe in this crazy day we live in and yet grow and expand and have some more creativity." Tuesday through Saturday she starts work at 9:45 a.m. or 11 a.m., sometimes at noon. Two evenings a week, she works until 8:15 p.m. "Those are good hours," Madeleine says. "You're not going to make lots of money. But you certainly have your energy and your sanity."

Madeleine uses her off-hours to explore business opportunities as a makeup artist. She may work part-time in a salon, or become a wedding consultant, or even assist a fashion photographer. Because she is giving herself time to explore all the options, "I find that all of a sudden I'm getting really excited about work every day," she says.

**To everything, a season.** At Arthur Andersen & Co., an interesting scheduling twist gives full-time employees a taste of working part-time for part of the year. According to Kathy Gallo, director of personnel matters, some offices are experimenting with a program that allows people to work a shorter week—only 32 hours—for 10 weeks in the summer. They make up the time over the year by putting in longer weeks— 48 hours each—for 10 weeks during the winter.

**Project Part-time.** These days, Rose Krupp-Ayala is part job-sharer and part contractor. Two days a week, she shares the duties of director of public affairs for the Los Angeles Chapter of the American Diabetes Association with Lynn Winter Gross. The rest of her time is often spent handling other projects, such as coordinating a walk-a-thon. "I'm in and out almost every day now," she admits. But that's only temporary.

She looks forward to the day she completes her project work and can go back to spending more time with her two daughters, ages 5 and 21 months. "I can stand to work these heavy schedules for three months at a time, but I really prefer to work two days a week, possibly three."

## What makes part-time work?

If you've never worked part-time, you may find it difficult to scale down the responsibilities of a full-time job into fewer than 40 hours a week. But that's the first step. The second is sticking to your schedule. It's also a good idea to:

- **Remain flexible.** Many part-timers agree that flexibility is the key to retaining goodwill and professional status. "I take calls at home on the days I'm off," says

Beverly Dinan. "I have a computer at home so I can dial in for my E-mail. I feel I really need to be that flexible in order to have that respect reciprocated."

- **Ask for a trial period.** This is a built-in escape-hatch for you and your employer. Don't wait until the end of the period to evaluate your progress. Chart your productivity and issue status reports.

- **If you're looking for a part-time job, choose a flexible industry.** If you're just beginning to look for part-time work, industries such as retail offer workers "full-time" schedules that are less than 40 hours a week, with full benefits.

## What can trip you up?

There are always pitfalls. In the middle of a new arrangement, they can be difficult to see. Try to avoid these bad habits.

- **Trying to do a full-time job part-time.** You can't do it, so don't try. In the following chapter are guidelines for breaking your current job apart, task by task, to create a satisfying and workable part-time arrangement.

- **Accepting unsatisfactory salary or benefits.** Be sure to negotiate the salary and benefits you need up front. Salary and benefits are often prorated for part-time positions, so make sure you can afford to fill in the gaps in health care coverage. Even if you don't plan to work extra hours, be sure to agree upon a fair hourly compensation.

- **Getting stuck with core hours or "odd" hours.** While any number of schedules are possible, make sure you know what is acceptable at your company.

# Part-Time Careers

Many companies require part-timers to put in core hours (9 a.m. to 3 p.m., for example) during which they want full coverage. If you can't work in the evenings or on the weekend, don't pursue a career in retail or other industries that traditionally keep "odd" hours.

## Job sharing: Two heads are better than one

When it works, it works beautifully—this "marriage" of two professional partners who share the responsibilities of one job. Like any marriage, this variation on the part-time theme will take careful planning and more than a little chemistry.

Like part-time schedules, job-sharing arrangements can take several forms.

**Sharing everything.** "We work together on all projects," says Lynn Winter Gross, who shares the title of director of public affairs for the Los Angeles Chapter of the American Diabetes Association with Rose Krupp-Ayala. Although neither started out with the idea of sharing a job, both like the idea of retaining an interesting career with part-time hours so they can spend more time at home with their small children.

Rose comes in two days a week. Lynn works four. The end result? More than full-time coverage. Though it was difficult to sell the company on the idea initially, both partners believe the company has become the big winner.

"The company is covered no matter what happens," says Lynn. "When we started, Rose was pregnant and had to take some time off unexpectedly before her baby was born, so I came back to work full-time. If there had been one person in the job, I don't know what the company would have done. Train another person? When one of us goes on vacation, we make sure the other one is here to cover the job. In most jobs, when you're gone, you're gone."

That kind of coverage can only enhance media relations, a major part of the job. "Whenever we make calls to the media, we always direct them to call either one of us" reports Lynn. "Letters are signed that way. Whenever one of us makes a call, it goes into the file with a note. That way, the information is easily accessible to us or the rest of the staff. On the days when Rose is out, if a media call comes in and I'm not in the office, I can be reached at home." Constant communication—whether by telephone, note or in person—has been the key to a creative and productive partnership.

In fact, Rose and Lynn consider themselves such a "good duo" that they have every intention of continuing the partnership indefinitely. "There's something about being on the cutting edge that makes it kind of fun," says Rose. "Rather than stepping back, we're stepping forward."

**Dividing the duties.** Sometimes the nature of a job makes it possible—even preferable—to divide tasks and responsibilities, usually by project or client group. This type of team may perform more autonomously than the team that shares everything, but in most cases the partners still attend the same meetings and cocktail parties and can back each other whenever it is required.

With a toddler and another baby on the way, Susan Strawbridge envisioned turning her job as a product manager into a job-share. All she had to do was sell her supervisor.

"I was definitely the first in my position," she says. But breaking ground at Novell, Inc., didn't phase her. She got to work on a lengthy proposal covering every task and contingency situation she could imagine, and providing for a six-month trial period. She just needed one thing: a partner.

As luck would have it, Susan's former manager returned from maternity leave to find many of her own responsibilities had disappeared. Even though she was a full-time employee, she was a prime candidate to take on half of Susan's job.

# Part-Time Careers

According to plan, "We split the hours—two and a half days each, with an hour overlap on Wednesdays," Susan says. Based on her initial outline of the product features, the new partners decided to specialize in certain features. "Each one was almost a project in itself."

Unfortunately, just as they got off the ground as a team, their product line was sold. Although Susan will return from maternity leave to a different, part-time job, she is hopeful about forging a job-sharing arrangement in the future.

**A marriage of convenience.** Can two people who perform separate tasks be tagged job-sharers? Some companies prefer to link two part-timers in the same department as job-sharers for the purposes of head count. These "teams" function more like distant cousins than partners. But when head count is an issue, this arrangement makes each partner less vulnerable to the vagaries of corporate shifts.

When her boss' assistant needed to take on additional responsibilities, Helen Purdum donated some of her own. "I trained her to do a lot of the pension work and I focused on communications," the pension benefits specialist at Levi Strauss says. "At first, she would come to me as an adviser—when she had questions or ran into sticky situations." But soon, both women were working independently—each putting in 30 hours a week.

## What makes job-sharing work?

The right partner can make—or break—the arrangement. Should you look for a clone? Based on the experience of many teams, it's helpful to look for the three "C's": Compatibility, Chemistry and Communication.

- **Compatibility.** Look for someone with a similar workstyle, as well as similar values and expectations. Of course, you both should have the same level

148

of expertise. And it helps to have a track record working for the same company.

- **Chemistry.** That's not to say that you can't bring complementary skills to the team. The idea person and the organizer. The writer and the sales person. When two whole people blend their expertise and enthusiasm in one job, the result can be far more than the sum of two half-timers.

- **Communication.** Most proposals build in an hour or more a week for formal communication between job-sharers. But most successful teams go far beyond that—talking daily on the telephone, walking together at lunchtime, leaving each other voice mail and E-mail messages and copious written notes.

    "Since we were so familiar with the job and each others' work habits, we really didn't need the hour of formal communication," says Susan Strawbridge. "We used to walk at lunch. There are so many opportunities to talk."

## What can trip you up?

There are many cracks in the sidewalk for job-sharing partners who do not see eye-to-eye or bother to keep the lines of communication open.

- **The wrong partner.** "You're vulnerable if you have a partner who doesn't put in the effort, or who is very competitive—always trying to take credit," says Susan Strawbridge.

- **Communication breakdowns.** When you're working alone, you can keep everything "in your head." When you're working closely with someone else, that is never an option. Even if you're not a detail person, you'll have to devise special procedures to ensure that nothing falls through the cracks.

## Telecommuting: Taking work home

Known less commonly as "flex-place" or "work-at-home," telecommuting is a gift of the electronic age we live in. With a telephone and computer in almost every home, there are already nearly 15 million people working—full- or part-time— from a home office. Some may be just across town from their companies. Others are across the country. Customer-service agents, fund raisers, writers, computer programmers, market researchers and public relations professionals all find it a plus.

"When the kids want us to be involved in their activities, we get involved," says Larry Nash. For eight years, he has been "borrowing" time from his regular work days to volunteer at his children's school—and coming into the office a little earlier or staying later. Three years ago, he started telecommuting from home where his wife, Cathy, works part-time as an interior designer.

His home system allows him to tie into the Local Area Network at U S West, where he is a director of administration. "The networks aren't as busy in the off-hours, so I can get faster access to things. I'll spend a little time on it again tonight. Because of the cooperation and understanding I've gotten from my boss and the company, I'm a much more productive—and happier—employee, says Larry.

**The long-distance supervisor.** How effective can a supervisor be long-distance? Many companies are still reluctant to find out. But many of those that have tried the arrangement are satisfied with the results. In fact, one supervisor working from a home office 3,000 miles away may be more accessible than another just down the hall, but with a hectic travel schedule.

"The people on my staff actually feel like they talk to me more when I'm in Maine than they do when I'm in California," says Karen Dowell, who manages 14 people working in California from her home office on Deer Isle off the coast of Maine. "It's just a matter of being very responsive."

The manager of technical publications, documentation and marketing communications for PeopleSoft, a San Francisco Bay Area software company, makes it a point to be available to answer specific questions and provide support. Still, on an average day, she spends less than two hours on the phone with staff members.

"We make a point to hire self-managing people," she says. "Once they understand their job and what we expect of them, they just do it. Basically it's the difference between having an administrative report and a manager report."

The company's dynamic growth requires Karen to be in touch constantly—online using electronic mail, on the phone, and, less frequently, in person. Following every two weeks in Maine, she spends one in California. She gladly trades geographical flexibility for longer hours. A typical day begins no later than 8 a.m. "before the office in California wakes up" and winds down at about 8 p.m. (standard quitting time on the West Coast.) Although she is probably more productive in her office over the garage than she would be in an office at corporate headquarters, there are some non-standard interruptions.

"Things are a little bit different here," she says. Her dog, Mac, may add his two-cents to a conference call. She may stop work to chat with the Federal Express delivery man about his vacation. On rare days, she may walk on the beach or take the kayak out, if the tide is right.

"I'm not ready to change anything," she says. "I'm having too much fun."

**Telecommuting from the field.** A fully equipped office in a car—complete with phone, fax and laptop computer—is just around the corner. But laptop technology is already getting Arthur Andersen executives out into the field on a more regular basis.

In an effort to reduce overhead and encourage more client contact, the consulting firm has equipped a third of its professional work force with laptop computers. Now, *anywhere* is an office. Executives can dial up the company's in-house computer and take care of any type of business.

## What makes telecommuting work?

Some people will have a hard time working at home, whether it's 30 miles from the office or 3,000 miles away. You need to be a bit of an entrepreneur to make it work.

- **Plenty of motivation.** It's up to you to get out of bed and on the telephone or in front of the computer every morning. With no one looking over your shoulder, you have to set your own schedule.

- **A separate office.** The only way to do battle with the multitude of distractions at home is to shut them out—behind the door of a separate room, or at least a partitioned space you vow to use only for work.

- **The right stuff.** In addition to comfortable furniture, you'll need a telephone and computer. Voicemail and E-mail make a good communications duo. Some telecommuters can do without a printer and run out to the photocopier. Others would be wise to invest in a complete set-up. You and your supervisor can decide.

## What can trip you up?

When you're out of sight, you can't afford to be out of mind, especially if you're a supervisor.

- **Fading out of sight.** "You can't assume that people are going to remember that you're there," say Karen Dowell. "You always have to go that extra step to make sure that your opinions and ideas are heard. If you're constantly giving status reports or seeding information out there, it shows that you are being productive. And if you're remote, you always have to try harder."

- **Using a work-at-home arrangement as a substitute for childcare.** You may be able to work "odd" hours when your children are sleeping or sick. Beyond that, you should arrange for childcare, just as you would if you were going in to an office.

   "You have to be very careful not to use any kind of flexible work arrangement as a childcare situation," advises Cathy Fowler of U S West. "It's not fair to you, or the company. Or the kids."

- **Not having a "Plan B."** What happens if the company goes out of business, or is sold and you find yourself in a remote location without a job? It happened to Karen Dowell and her advice is simply "Be prepared. You have to feel that you can always start on your own again if you lose that security."

## The temporary solution

There's one more option in use by a growing number of professionals, according to the U.S. Department of Labor— temporary help services. This booming industry has grown at a rate of 20 percent every year during the past 20. Once the last resort for administrative and clerical workers, today it is the choice of an increasing number of professionals—including lawyers and doctors—who want to supplement their incomes, beef up their resumes or simply "keep in touch" after retirement.

153

# Part-Time Careers

"I think that temping is the best way to find a permanent job," insists Linda Nydick. After a two-week assignment at L'Oreal's Corporate Scientific Division, "things just seemed to click," she remembers. Over the following months she also worked in the human resources department. "I was able to show myself off to my best advantage." Finally, when she filled in for a woman in another department who had decided not to return from maternity leave, she was asked to stay on permanently.

Diane Thrailkill has seen the same thing happen many times. "I always compare what happens on the job to a romance. When the chemistry is right, companies make room for you," she says. And if the relationship is not made in heaven, you'll have the opportunity to find out sooner, rather than too late, Diane says.

As a "professional temp" herself for the past six years, Diane admits she has become something of an expert on what she considers a very satisfying lifestyle. In fact, for the past two years, she has conducted a three-hour seminar on the subject for displaced workers looking for full-time work as well as anyone interested in the temping as a permanent lifestyle. She is also the author of *Temp by Choice* (Career Press, Spring, 1994).

As a former technical trainer, Diane knows 30 software packages, so she can typically earn from $14 to $18 dollars an hour as a temp. "If you put in a 45-hour week (that includes five hours of time-and-a-half) at $14 an hour for 48 weeks a year, that's almost $32,000. At $18 an hour, it's $41,000," she says. "You're not getting rich, but you're able to pay bills."

While there is a great deal of flexibility—certainly you are free to pick and choose your assignments—you may have to make some scheduling concessions. "I prefer a week-long assignment," Diane admits. "However, with the recession, at least in New York, the day-to-day stuff has really dried up. Companies are making do if somebody is out for a day or two.

So I've had to take longer assignments—from two weeks to two months—in order to stay employed."

## What makes temping work?

In order to succeed in this kind of market you have to have definable skills and an entrepreneurial spirit. Think of yourself as a small business, constantly marketing your skills to agencies and employers in exchange for money.

- **Have a plan.** "Temping lends itself to so many different things," Diane says. "I had a computer consulting business and, boy, when you first start up, there is no money coming in. You have these huge blocks of time when you're trying to set up appointments. During times like those, it's great to be a temp and get an hourly rate."

  You might decide to temp to free up large blocks of time for a personal project, escape the stresses and politics of a hectic profession or learn more about another industry.

- **Use your time on the job wisely.** Seize every opportunity to learn something new, and when you receive praise for your work on a job, ask your supervisor to pass it along to your temporary agency.

"I encourage people who are just starting out to register with one or more large agencies to learn the ropes," says Diane. "But I think there is more flexibility, in terms of higher rates of pay, with smaller companies," says Diane.

Other temps report that smaller agencies often will take time to understand and accommodate your needs. If you have a special skill or field of expertise, register with one or agencies that specialize in placing professionals in your field.

Because you are performing on the job all the time, you must keep your skills sharpened. Most agencies test the proficiency of temps and some may make software tutorials available or arrange training on the software programs commonly used by their larger clients.

If you truly enjoy the lifestyle, don't let anybody paint you as a victim. "Temps aren't people who are settling for less, they're settling for something different. It may not be mainstream, but the people who are successful are taking charge and running their own small businesses," says Diane.

Temps have rights, too. Agencies and companies may not always be up front about the "fine print," so you have to make it your business to protect yourself from being exploited.

"Most people don't know that if you work for a company for 1,000 hours that you're entitled under the Federal IRS codes to have the same benefits as regular employees, under certain circumstances," Diane says. She admits that some agencies and companies get around this by hiring long-term temps, firing them just before the 1,000 hours are up—and then re-hiring them.

Some large temporary agencies offer health care insurance and vacation pay to some temps. Temporary agencies pay into unemployment. You may be able to collect against them if they don't provide work for you. Ask about the policies.

## What can trip you up?

When you invest in a lifestyle that lacks benefits and opportunities for promotion, you have to be careful.

- **Getting stuck in underearning.** Can you afford to earn $7 an hour? If not, beware of climbing aboard a treadmill that won't be easy to dismount. If you lack skills to earn more, it's better to find a way to go back to school.

- **Becoming part of a "people mill."** The large agencies are more visible, so they must offer better opportunities, right? Maybe. Interview agencies as carefully as they interview you.

Many temporary workers complain large agencies are impersonal and pay lower wages than smaller agencies. Large agencies often bid on long-term packages for large companies. Once they get the contract, those agencies must hire people who will work for the lower rates they negotiated.

# A plan of action

Hopefully by now, you've decided that one of these options feels "right." If so it's time to begin the negotiation process that will place you in your new workstyle.

## Chapter 9

# Part-time corporate: How to work it out

When her son was 3, Holly Angus was able to get approval to begin working three days a week so she could spend more time with him. Her department had just been reorganized into two teams. As the only part-timer, her job as marketing production manager turned into a "floating" position.

Now, even though she is the most experienced person in her department, "I pick up a lot of odd jobs," Holly says. "When the teams are up to their eyeballs working on a promotion, they can't stop what they're doing to put together a little survey. So that's the kind of thing I handle. I don't have a job description. It's such a hybrid thing."

The department is temporarily understaffed, adding to a production-by-crisis atmosphere. Much of Holly's time is spent answering questions and readjusting her schedule to take on last-minute projects. "I know what's on my schedule, so I can plan my time. But all of a sudden there's a survey that has to be in the mail tomorrow. That bumps everything else back."

Has her job become less satisfying? "I'd have to say so," she admits. "I feel like I'm very much on a 'mommy track' now. One person in the department is working 60 to 70 hours a week and the company is holding her up as a model. But if you have kids, you can't do that. For now, I'm just so grateful to be able to work part-time that I'll do anything they want."

At 61, Mary Lou Sweeney has her sights set on retirement. When she realized she wouldn't be able to afford to retire in California on her own a few years ago, she began to scout around for the next best thing. It turned out to be Sequim (pronounced "Skwim"), a community on Washington's Olympic Peninsula. Now, rather than put her plans on hold, she wants to move and keep on working—as a telecommuter.

With a computer, modem and electronic mail, Mary Lou could perform her job as a commission accountant from Sequim as well as she could from her desk in Silicon Valley—without the people she serves noticing any change in service. "I think it would work," she says. "But I have to sell it."

While she may well be breaking new ground in the accounting department, Mary Lou is banking that the time is ripe for proposing new working options at Sun Microsystems. Like many other companies, the high-tech giant is looking closely at staffing levels and relying on contractors to fill gaps.

The only potential glitch in her plan may be benefits. If she cannot convince the company to retain her as a full-time employee, she may lose health care coverage at a time when she can least afford it. Still, she's hopeful. Every day she punches in her password—"94sequim"—and polishes her proposal. "We'll see how much goodwill I can muster," she says.

## Negotiating new options

Let's say you've developed a close working relationship with your supervisor. Like Holly and Mary Lou, you've got a track record for being one of the department's most consistent performers. But you have personal plans that would require you to work fewer hours—at least for a while. You've been thinking it through during your morning runs and you've got an idea that you think just might work. You agonize over whether you should bring it up at an informal lunch, or schedule an official meeting to present your proposal.

Even in the most "friendly" of climates, renegotiating a full-time job to part-time, or proposing a job-share or telecommuting arrangement, is a process that you should take as seriously and plan for as carefully as you would any major move in your career.

## Think of it as a business proposal

Before you present your position, there are things you should be clear about. Can you afford it? Are you willing to take on special projects or work extra hours if necessary? Can you be promoted?

You'll also have to anticipate the concerns your supervisor is likely to have. Will co-workers be able to reach you on your days off? Or be envious of your "special treatment?" What about meetings and trade shows? How will the company benefit from this change? What happens if it doesn't work out?

As you conduct your research and fine-tune your plan, you'll discover there are few givens. Is your supervisor the right person to approach? Probably (but not always). Can you sell a proposal if you've only been with the company a few months? Probably not (but maybe).

The time you spend preparing a thorough proposal will be time well spent. The more bargaining power you can bring to the table—in terms of your own flexibility and benefits the arrangement will offer the company—the more money, status and job satisfaction you're likely to walk away with. Ready to get started? Let's begin at the beginning.

## Are you in the right place?

Take a hard, objective look at your current company or the company you are interviewing. How "family-friendly" is it? Are there innovative policies already in practice? Or are employees afraid to use them?

If you're relatively new to the company, the reaction of future co-workers and management will be telling. If co-workers are openly frustrated and managers seem glib about work/family issues, you'll have a tough road to travel. A "flextime" policy may allow only one hour leeway on the normal schedule. Companies that are actively evaluating and reworking work/family policies are more likely to accept new solutions.

**What's on paper?** Is there a formal, written policy for flexible working arrangements? Fewer than 40 percent of the companies participating in a Catalyst study on flexible jobs reported the existence of a formal policy. That's not necessarily bad news. Some companies prefer to keep things informal.

"There is something to be said for having policies formalized enough so that each party has the same expectations," admits Cathy Fowler of U S West. "But if you start mapping things out too much, you can lose something. Rather than the exception, we want flexibility to be part of the fabric of our corporate culture." Since 1987, when employees resoundingly requested flexible work/family support programs, the company has encouraged flexibility. Job-sharing, compressed work weeks, flexible scheduling, part-time work, flextime and telecommuting are all viable options.

Companies that promote a team approach are more fertile ground for spawning job-sharers and self-managing employees who do well in flexible arrangements. Companies that value innovation tend to be more comfortable with change and more interested in results.

**Does top management say it's OK?** Bausch and Lomb's commitment to flexibility extends far beyond its Rochester, N.Y., headquarters. Manufacturing sites are encouraged to adopt flexibility whenever possible. The company posts job-shares internally and, when necessary, advertises outside the company to fill job-share openings.

Are people at all levels encouraged to participate in flexible programs, or are they taboo for managers, or men, or salaried professionals who want to "get ahead"?

Not at Hewlett Packard. There are 585 regular part-timers working throughout the United States—40 in supervisory roles and more than half in salaried positions.

**Strategy: Test the idea.** If a written policy is in place, but you're not sure your supervisor would support it, "test" the idea in casual conversation. Is your curiosity met with a strongly negative reaction? Or does the supervisor seem to be uninformed about flexible arrangements? If so, offer to get a copy of the written policy from the human resources department so he or she can review it at leisure.

## Seven steps to a winning proposal

If you've decided you have a better-than-average chance for selling a new working arrangement or are simply challenged by the idea of breaking new ground in your company, there are seven key steps to the process of getting approval.

## 1. Examine your financial situation and benefits

Use the company's written policy as your guide to determining what kind of health care coverage you can receive on a part-time basis. You may be able to shift your coverage to your spouse's plan. If not, you may have to work more hours to receive full benefits.

Most companies prorate salary and benefits—including health care insurance, vacation and sick and personal days—based on hours worked. Some are generous, offering full benefits at 15 or 20 hours a week. Others have tightened the purse strings and require even full-time employees to contribute to the total cost of their plan. As a part-timer, you may be able to purchase the remainder of your health care package at a rate far below what you would pay for an individual policy. Know your options, so you can be sure you'll be able to afford what you're proposing.

## 2. Decide which hours you want to work

Can you restructure your full-time job to fit them? Start by keeping a detailed record of your daily activities. What tasks can you delegate? Can you share your job with someone else? Are there seasonal slumps? Could you get more done by working at home? Your personal needs and the type of job you have will determine which flexible option you choose.

## 3. Build goodwill—by doing a good job

Make yourself indispensable. This is good advice for any professional, especially in today's climate. But for anyone seeking a flexible working arrangement, it is important leverage. Acquire all the skills and knowledge you can. Build support among your peers and subordinates.

With what she calls "malice of forethought," Mary Lou Sweeney has worked hard to develop competence using the latest technology and to develop a reputation as a dependable, responsive team player. She'll use it all in her bid for a telecommuting arrangement. "I've proven myself when I handled four desks during a 'week from hell.' There's no reason that I can't fill in during a crisis from Sequim (Wash.). Anything I need can be E-mailed to me."

## 4. Look for success stories

Scout around for informal situations like the one you want to propose that may have evolved in other corners of the company. If they've been successful, learn how. Listen for details about productivity gains, enhanced customer relationships and additional coverage that you can use in your own proposal.

## 5. Decide who decides

Who has the power to approve your proposal? Would someone else be more sympathetic to your situation?

Rose Krupp-Ayala and Lynn Winter Gross were getting nowhere proposing a job-share to an interim director at the Los Angeles Chapter of the American Diabetes Association. "He had a lot of objections. Mostly that it would be too confusing to the staff and that everybody else would want to do it, too," remembers Lynn.

With the help of a consultant, the duo revised the proposal and took it to the interim director's boss. "He had remarried and had a baby with his new wife. He could see what it was like for his wife to want to be working with a child at home. So he was interested in trying it," she reports.

## 6. Draft your proposal

If flexible programs are encouraged in your company, there may be an established procedure you are expected to follow in presenting your proposal.

While the Laguna Salada School District enthusiastically encourages job-sharing, it allows no more than one team per 10 teachers in each school. According to John Perry, director of personnel, prospective job-sharing teams must have their principal's approval and submit a comprehensive proposal for review by a job-sharing committee to ensure that the needs of students—as well as their parents and other teachers—are taken into consideration.

If there is no set format and you anticipate resistance, hire a consultant to suggest a format, review your proposal and help you answer objections. As you write and revise, trusted colleagues may also be enlisted to offer suggestions and play devil's advocate. Your presentation might follow this format:

**Introduce yourself.** Begin by reminding your supervisor and company of your past accomplishments and consistent performance. Bring up facts that play in your favor—you've been with the company for eight years and are familiar with the functions of several departments, you have received recognition for high productivity, most of your work requires little interaction with others. Wherever you can, use real numbers to quantify the expenses.

**Write a detailed job description for your new job.** Your goal is to structure a position that will be satisfying to you and make good business sense to your supervisor.

Using your current job description, check off duties that best suit your skills and are most interesting and challenging to you. Put a star beside those which you know to be top priorities for the company. This is your core—and your security. Decide which other tasks on your list can be delegated or reassigned. Which might be eliminated.

Show how you'll complete your tasks working within the schedule you're requesting. It's important to stress flexibility. Can you be reached at home on your days off? How often will you come into the office if you're telecommuting? Set up a schedule for reporting on the status of your projects.

**Show how it will work—from your supervisor's perspective.** Your supervisor will want to know what might slip through the cracks. So answer every contingency you can think of. What emergencies might arise? If you are a supervisor, who will answer questions when you are not available? If you're sharing a job, who will attend conferences? Paint sample scenarios, if you think it will help.

Make this section of your proposal as lengthy as you feel you must to cover every objection your supervisor is likely to have. The initiative you demonstrate in attending to the details is sure to make a favorable impression.

Also, show how the new arrangement could be more beneficial to the goals of the department. Point out that two people sharing one job can cover for each other during vacations. Talk about how working at home without interruptions can make you more productive and save the company the overhead of an office and equipment. But be careful not to over-promise.

**Suggest a trial period.** Propose it as a safety net for your supervisor. But know that it is also an ideal opportunity for you to fix all the glitches you couldn't anticipate when you wrote the original proposal.

**Salary and benefits.** Make specific, but reasonable, requests for compensation. Remember that you represent a valuable business asset to your employer. You'll be forfeiting money and benefits to work flexible hours, so negotiate an arrangement that is equitable for both you and the company.

Anticipate issues such as: How will you be compensated for working overtime? Will you be entitled to the annual bonus? How will salary increases be handled? Commissions? Other expenses?

## 7. Present your proposal

Again, format is important. Will your supervisor feel more comfortable carefully reviewing a written proposal or having you present your arguments orally?

**Strategy: Choose the right time.** For you and your supervisor. You won't get far if you appear in a panic after your latest childcare arrangement has fallen through or when your boss is under deadline pressure. Choose a time when you've reached a clear decision about your own career and have done the necessary homework.

As always, it pays to keep an ear to the grapevine for news of an impending reorganization or acquisition that may give you an opening—or make a flexible working arrangement more vulnerable.

"I decided to strike while the iron appeared to be hot—and it worked," says Holly. "Part-time had been in the back of my mind even before my son was born. But my previous supervisor made it clear that he didn't think it would be workable for me," she says. In the midst of a department reorganization, her new supervisor stopped her in the hall and informally asked her how she saw her position evolving. "I said, 'I see myself going part-time,'" she remembers. "He said, 'I don't think there should be a problem with that.'"

**Sitting down at the negotiating table.** If your proposal is accepted at face value, you're in. But chances are there will be a few questions, objections and points of contention. Don't give up. Negotiate.

The key is to be accommodating, without giving away too much. Take time to go over points calmly. If you are trying to break new ground in your company or department, what you are proposing is likely to make your supervisor uncomfortable. Some bosses may be inflexible and unwilling to consider a change. Don't issue ultimatums. Stress your interest in give-and-take. Try-it-and-see. Demonstrate your willingness to work together to achieve mutual goals.

This is the time to listen carefully. Are there ways to answer objections by fine-tuning the proposal? Or is your supervisor simply stonewalling you? If that is the case, can you gain support from someone in human resources without risking your current position?

Negotiating is art—and a tricky process if you're not used to it. *Getting to Yes*, by Roger Fisher and William Ury, is one of the best books on the market. But there are many others that can help you feel more comfortable with working out the details of an equitable package. Then take time to practice. Family members and friends can help you role-play.

## Working it out—on the job

You've sold your proposal. Enjoy your extra time. But don't relax at work. Especially during the initial trial period you've established, it's important to put in some extra effort to make sure your arrangement starts successfully.

**Be prepared for staff resistance.** According to Lynn Winter Gross, "The staff was angry," when she started sharing a job with Rose Krupp-Ayala. "They thought I was getting away with something. I said 'I'm taking a cut in pay to do this.' We both had to keep explaining that the job was being done. Nothing was falling through the cracks."

**Communicate.** Good communication will cover a lot of ground with co-workers. Let everyone in on your new hours, how to handle procedures and how you can be reached in an emergency. Always clear up loose ends before you go home each day, especially if you're not coming in the next day.

**Stay visible—and accessible.** If you're a manager, establish a weekly routine for your staff and stay up-to-date on their progress. Never give staff members cause to go over your head for support.

**Don't apologize.** If people complain that you weren't in your office when they tried to reach you, ask to set an appointment. Nobody can be in their office every minute of the working day.

**Keep growing.** Set personal goals that will help you meet your professional goals. Follow trends in your industry and plan your career path just as carefully as you would if you were working full-time.

## Six steps to finding a part-time job

If you've decided to change companies or want to find a satisfying part-time job in another field, expect your search to take as long—or longer—than a search for a full-time job. The following steps will get you started:

**1. Set guidelines for the salary and benefits you'll accept.** How much do you need to earn to pay for childcare and benefits? Can you afford the commute? If you're moving into a more formal environment, will you need to invest in more appropriate work attire?

**2. Make contact(s).** Tell everyone you know that you are looking for a part-time job. At professional and social gatherings ask other professionals about opportunities for flexible work arrangements in their companies. If you're changing careers, conduct information interviews. Remember that most jobs are filled through referrals.

**3. Look for full- and part-time positions.** It's a long shot, but you may be able to sell an employer on making a full-time position a job-share. You'll need a partner. It's often easier to get a job-sharing arrangement approved if one partner already works for the company. Request a job description and put together a proposal.

**4. Check job lines, job boards and job fairs regularly.** Many companies, as well as government agencies, professional associations and colleges and universities update bulletin board and telephone listings weekly.

**5. Identify the right kind of company.** Call the human resources department and inquire about work/family benefits and flexible work arrangements. Small companies may be more open to adapting work schedules.

# Part-Time Careers

Larger companies with highly visible "family-friendly" policies tend to promote flexible work schedules as part of their overall approach to personnel issues. Companies that allow you to choose benefits "cafeteria-style" are often more receptive to flexible work schedules.

- **For telecommuting.** Look for companies that offer project-oriented work, such as research, writing, computer programming and management training.
- **For part-time.** Look for high-stress occupations. Part-time schedules can help workers reduce burnout in such fields as corrections, social work and customer service.
- **For job-sharing.** Nonprofit companies, such as libraries, associations, universities and human service organizations often employ a large number of women and, so, may be more open to a variety of flexible arrangements.

**6. Have patience.** Whether you are negotiating a new part-time job or renegotiating your full-time position to part-time or a job-share, the opportunities are increasing. Go for it.

# Part 4

# Coming home: Creating a home-based business (and a more satisfying life)

*"They always say that time changes things.
But actually, you have to change them yourself."*
—Andy Warhol

# Chapter 10

# The pleasures and perils of becoming the boss

"When I first started out as a marketing communications consultant, a consultant was a person who couldn't get a job, or hold a job. There was a real stigma to it," remembers Donna Wotton. "People weren't comfortable working with someone they didn't *own*. I happened into a couple of situations that were very long-term and employment-like. But I can't count the number of times those people bribed me to come on staff. I just didn't want to give up my independence and my choices," she says.

Now that she runs Unconventional Promotions, a successful meeting/event planning business, Donna finds that the pendulum has swung the other way for an increasing number of home-based professionals like herself.

## What's changed?

Organizations grappling with the high cost of "head count" are more than willing to pay handsomely for outside expertise.

In the pinch of downsizing, there is plenty of opportunity for the home-based business owner working on a project-by-project basis. What's more, a world tiring of deadwood and mass-produced ideas is ready to welcome the maverick professional who gets satisfaction from going the extra mile.

"All of my clients are fairly long-term," Donna says. "They love having us at their disposal. They don't have to bring us up to speed. We already know all the players. They dump a project on us and we go do it. It's practically invisible to them after that. They attend a couple of meetings to make sure we're on target. We process all the paperwork through their systems and use their forms. We don't get paid unless we complete the project to their satisfaction."

Whether you're aching to call your own shots or simply want to arrange your work so you can spend more time with your family—the time is ripe for making your move.

## Caveat entrepreneur

Home-based professionals are the first to tell you the lifestyle is not for everyone. For every day that you're still drinking coffee in your bathrobe at noon, there may be two when you're still burning the midnight oil, long after midnight. Will you work next week? Will you have money for taxes next month? Will you still be in business next year?

It's all up to you. That's the blessing and the curse. You set the work schedule. You chart the goals. You manage the cash flow and promote yourself in a competitive marketplace. And it's up to you to keep doing it, day after day.

If you have the right blend of faith and persistence, this lifestyle will become its own reward and there will come a day, probably early on, when you know a moment of truth. You will never go back "inside." The following stories of home-based entrepreneurs are proof-positive:

# Part-Time Careers

## Unconventional values

"I got started the way most people get started—by leaving a job," remembers Donna Wotton.

Nine years ago, she was still on the fast track. She was an advertising manager for a Silicon Valley electronics company with six years of experience, and a dangerous case of burnout. "From the time I was 21 until I was 27, I dedicated my life to work," she says. "I was raised with this wonderful Puritan work ethic that you have to work and work and work until everyone approves. So I was a seven-day-a-week, twelve-hour-a-day workaholic. I had achieved what I thought I wanted, and it wasn't what I thought it was going to be. All I did was manage the budget and other people's baggage. I was doing less of what I wanted to do, with more and more heartache. I just had to pull the plug."

So when her company had a layoff, she surprised everyone by volunteering.

"It was an act of self-preservation," she insists. "When my friends said, 'What are you going to do?' I said, 'I don't know.' But I said it with glee. All I knew was that this nonsense was going to be over, and I didn't feel any pressure to decide on what my fate was going to be."

Donna's courage and confidence had roots in her upbringing. When she was 12, her father left a good job as a vice president of New York Telephone Company to start a sailing center. "He risked everything," she remembers. "We went from being 'poor little rich kids' in a big, fancy neighborhood to poor kids trying to hang onto a house in a fancy neighborhood." Donna and her sisters helped run what is now a thriving business with multiple locations on the East Coast. And the seeds of an entrepreneur were sown.

With no intention of working for awhile after her own departure from the corporate world, Donna remembers, "I would call my friends in the middle of the day and say, 'Do you want to come for dinner?' I hadn't seen my friends in months. I hadn't done anything in the middle of a week in years. I worked out every day. I had this fabulous garden. I read trashy novels. I went to the beach. I went out at night. I did whatever I pleased."

After three and half months, former business associates started seeking her out for freelance work. "I started dabbling in that," she admits. "I was only working about 20 hours a week. I could still do what I wanted, but I had a little money coming in." Meanwhile, she began interviewing for full-time jobs similar to the one she left—and rejecting all the job offers she received.

"There was something keeping me from taking another job," she says. With her freelance "dabbling" now taking up 40 hours a week, she remembers, "One day I woke up and said, 'Maybe you can perpetuate this for a while and not have to go back to work.' But, it was two years before I admitted, 'OK, this is a job.' "

When a friend at Apple Computer asked her to step in and handle a series of trade shows on short notice a few years later, a new business was born. "I would be gone a week at a time here and there, and it was more there than here. After about a year of doing those events, I weaned my advertising clients to other people."

As the owner of Unconventional Promotions for the past six years, Donna plans and coordinates a wide range of corporate events—trade shows, sales conferences, product introductions, press tours, hospitality suites. She takes on more than 20 events a year with the help of two coordinators and a loose coalition of self-employed graphic designers, presentation and exhibit designers and technical experts skilled in audiovisual, staging and computer networking.

It's a working arrangement that works well for the clients and the contractors. "I put together the right team based on what the client needs," Donna explains. "Clients get top-notch talent for exactly what they need, without having to keep these people on staff. We get to pick and choose what projects we want. If we're overloaded, we'll bring in another co-ordinator."

For events such as a three-day meeting designed to unite senior-level Apple Computer executives with senior-level press and industry analysts from around the country, the team begins meeting six months ahead of time to devise elaborate demonstrations of unreleased product and create technically intensive, hour-long presentations for each of 20 speakers.

"We're the communications hub," says Donna, who has two to five events in progress at all times. "We keep every-body on track and make sure everybody meets their dead-lines."

In the on-again-off-again world of event planning, Donna protects herself from burnout by using her downtime to re-charge. She takes six weeks of vacation a year and is a relentless advocate for her friends in danger of taking their work too seriously.

"I'm not a very good victim anymore," she laughs. "I'm so used to making my own decisions about what I do with my time and myself and my interests, that even if I went back on the inside, I think it would be more frustrating for whoever I worked for."

## Success—by design

"It's amazing how life sometimes seems to happen to you," muses Diane Hyde. But although the success of her Diane H line of handcrafted jewelry and clothing may continue to amaze her, she can't deny that it was her drive and persis-tence as a businesswoman that made it happen. Throughout her life, she has grown accustomed to reinventing herself through her interests.

In what she calls a "metamorphosis," Diane advanced from production assistant to graphic designer and illustrator to entrepreneur by absorbing every bit of knowledge she could find and using it to develop the skills that would further her goals. Although she was successfully freelancing as a designer and illustrator, she insists that the pivotal step to creating her current business was accepting her last full-time job.

As assistant director for Dynamic Graphic Educational Foundation (DGEF) in Peoria, Ill., she regularly traveled across the country to market hands-on workshops for professional graphic designers and visual communicators. "Every time I went somewhere, I was compelled to look at creative things and gather ideas. I had a sketchbook with me all the time and when I would see clothing or jewelry, usually hand-made or one-of-a-kind, I would either sketch it or buy it or somehow imprint it upon my brain."

Finally, she tried her hand at making her first pieces, using a material called plaster-impregnated gauze that can be molded into free-form shapes when wet and then painted or used as a base for gluing on other items once it is dry.

"I'd wear them to work and everybody went crazy over them," Diane remembers. During the holidays, she did a booming business out of her office and soon afterward was selling her jewelry at some of the better art shows in the area.

"I got to the point where I was really frustrated working all day," she admits. "I could barely keep my mind on my work. All I could think about was what I wanted to make. It was time to make the jump. So I quit my job to pursue this full-time, to see where it was going to take me."

With the support of her husband, Cam, Diane set goals for managing and growing a very different kind of business venture. "Cam is a manager," she explains. "He loves that kind of organization. He would come up with questions I never would have thought to ask myself, such as 'How do you intend to market this?' 'How do you intend to have inventory on hand if you get an order?' 'What are your long-range plans?' I can't imagine anyone who could have helped catapult me into this better than he has. He allowed it to happen for me."

She used income from her part-time freelance illustration and borrowed from savings to create her initial inventory. After identifying suppliers through classified listings and advertising in selected trade magazines, she sat down with their catalogs and learned her next lesson. "I was overwhelmed at the minimums of beads and metal pieces and wires you have to order," she remembers. "In two minutes, you've already spent $500. I ordered very small amounts at first. It became a wish list instead of a purchase order."

Today, Diane's basement is a one-woman design studio and production facility. Although she occasionally farms out piece work, she admits she should be delegating more of the piece work and administrative tasks, so she can be free to do the work she loves—creating new products. "I have much more fun when everything is in its raw stage and the excitement of what's going to come out is on the horizon," she says.

Her latest project is in the works—a line of products imprinted with an illustration of the Greek goddess, Diana.

"This is the next big step to where I really want to go—to a bigger market. I love the images I create and I want to share them with everybody."

## Perfect pitch

There was a time when Rick Kelly* says he was too much of an elitist to suppose that he could turn from composing music to composing advertising copy.

"If the guy sitting next to me at the lunch counter told me he was studying business or advertising, I would have labeled him 'mercantile,' " he admits. "Advertising was part of our

* Not his real name.

mass idiot culture. The last thing I wanted to have anything to do with was that." But that was when he was in college. Rick found that maturity and practicality have a way of changing perceptions. And so began an interesting transition.

As a graduate student in music composition, "tired of having the rent plus $500," Rick began to face the economic reality of the career he was pursuing.

"Even though I had a fellowship, I realized that I wouldn't be able to make very much when I got a job. Did I want to spend my life at a university? Tenure track positions were fairly scarce, so every three to five years I'd have to go somewhere else. Would I be able to support a family? Probably not. Or at least not in the style I wanted. Since I grew up lower-middle class, I didn't have parents who could bail me out from slumming around as an artist." With this mind, Rick reluctantly left music. "I had no idea what I wanted to do. But at 28, I decided I'd better start doing it.

"My goal was to find something that was reasonably creative so I'd be interested, and reasonably lucrative." He worked part-time as a legal secretary and administrative manager and taught music lessons on the side while he studied the options.

A program offered through the Career Counseling Center at the University of California at Berkeley provided the key. Although Rick was skeptical of having a computer tell him what to do with his life, he agreed to take a battery of tests. One of them so strongly correlated his interests and abilities with the job of advertising executive, "it was almost off the chart," Rick remembers.

Putting aside his past prejudices, Rick took classes, gathered experience and developed a self-promotion brochure that would demonstrate his creative skills and answer any objections he might encounter as composer-turned-copywriter. In it, he wove what seem like opposing aptitudes together using a single concept—delivering the "perfect pitch."

179

# Part-Time Careers

Rick gained access into the world of advertising and spent several successful years in it, accumulating expertise with high-tech accounts.

The hectic pace and long hours also were taking their toll. "I was beginning to miss some of my creative endeavors, like having more time to write music and play gigs. It's hard to get home at 2 a.m. and have to get up early the next morning," he says. So after five years, "I engineered my departure."

As a freelancer, Rick has built a solid reputation with a mostly high-tech clientele. Recently he found time to begin working on a children's book of verse, although he admits it has been a challenge to steal the time away from his business to finish it.

"There are some people who are constitutionally incapable of making the kind of compromise that I did," Rick admits. "It has been exactly the compromise I envisioned. It's been lucrative and creative. It has served me very well."

These days, he is philosophical about this practicality. "You can get where you want to be in your life through a series of steps. I may find myself back writing music again in a way that works for me and not as some embittered underpaid professor at Iowa State who didn't get tenure for the third time in a row."

## A family affair

Disillusionment with the economic prospects of a career in music also launched Jill Hartnell on a very different career path.

After a year of college, she set her sights on business school. But while she was waiting to be accepted, she applied to several companies and was hired by Mutual Life Insurance of Ottawa, Canada. She entered its computer training program and stayed on.

"In many ways, I got a better education there than I could have gotten at a university," she says. "They had excellent facilities. I didn't learn bad habits because they did everything right." She continued to attend classes throughout her five years with the company, moving on to become a customer account manager for Data Design Associates in Sunnyvale, Calif.

When Data Design merged with a company called Integral in Walnut Creek, Calif., she found herself serving a whole new set of corporate objectives. It wasn't long before Jill and her husband, Kevin McConnen, were talking seriously of forming their own consulting company. With two former colleagues from Data Design, they inaugurated Oasis Consulting in 1990.

In this new venture, Jill saw the opportunity to combine satisfying, high-paying work with raising a family. "I knew that a family was going to be my top priority and that I would not want to work full-time," she says. "Finding another, part-time job was not an option for me. Doing what I'm doing now, I can work part-time or full-time, depending on the workload. And I earn a lot of money for the time I do spend working."

With 1-year-old Casey now on the scene, the plan seems to be working beautifully. "I pay for full-time day-care right now," Jill says. "But I only have him in it when I need to. If it turns out that we're not busy, we may put him in only two or three days a week, or for a shorter time during the day."

Like any working mother, Jill has taken on a busier daily routine. On a typical work day, she feeds and dresses Casey and takes him to day-care before getting on the telephone to follow up with clients and keep in touch with her Oasis colleagues. Like her partners, she often juggles up to five customers at a time—working on projects and answering questions. "Each of us handles our own work, everything from A to Z, from getting the business and doing the work, to invoicing and following up." The group comes together for industry conferences and other key events.

# Part-Time Careers

The company's loose structure is designed to enhance the independence of each partner while leveraging promotion for the entire group. While modifying a company's general ledger system, for example, one partner is often able to scout opportunities for another who specializes in accounts payable.

Travel is the only sticky subject. While she was helping launch Oasis and build the business, Jill didn't mind spending as much as 80 percent of her time away from home. She scaled it down to 50 percent while she was pregnant. But after her son was born, she set a strict limit on the amount and frequency of the time she will spend away from him. "I don't want to leave him more than once a month," she insists. "Ideally it would be less than that. I've been able to stick to one trip a month and they've been two or three days each time."

What travel takes away is more than made up for by the flexibility of a work-at-home situation. In fact, Jill was back to work a week after Casey born—working part-time in her home office while he slept. "The flexibility has been wonderful. I have the best of both worlds."

## Let them eat cake

What began as a hobby for Marie Sims long ago turned into a profitable business. These days, she enjoys sweet success—baking and decorating cakes for all occasions in her own kitchen.

The interest of a secretary at the private school her children attended sparked her venture. "One day, she said, 'Why don't you sell your cakes?' " remembers Marie. "She was my first customer."

Now her children have grown. And so has the business. Like many home-based business owners, she finds it's either "feast or famine." Although she works an average of about 15 hours a week, during a feast week, Marie may work as many as 50 hours—balancing kitchen logistics with customer relations.

"Some weekends you think, 'There's no way I'll be able to get all this done!' But it always works out," she says. "It's that old deal about putting one foot in front of the other when you want to get across the room." By now, she has learned to take the complex logistics in stride, sometimes baking and freezing cakes, making the roses and cutting and wrapping platform boards a few days ahead of time, if necessary.

While she can never accurately predict the wedding season each year, the traditional holiday seasons tend to be quiet. Throughout the year, she may handle a variety of projects, such as helping one woman "fool" her friends and relatives into thinking she's always slaving away over homemade goodies. "She never wants them to look decorated," Marie laughs.

Comfortable with her success, she is also grateful for the challenges she's faced in running her business. While she admits that those first couple of projects caused her a few sleepless nights, she is quick to add, "After a while, you realize you can do more than you ever thought you could do. That's a neat feeling."

## A career makeover

"When I was growing up in North Carolina back in the '60s, careers for women really weren't discussed," remembers Trish Adams. "Maybe you'd be a teacher or maybe you'd be a nurse. Or maybe you'd just get married and have kids and stay home."

So, after two years of college, she and her first husband settled into what would be the first of many cities on his company's transfer circuit—Boise, Idaho. A few years later, and just a few courses shy of completing her degree in education, Trish and her husband were transferred to Denver. By this time, they had started a family. So Trish put off school and dabbled in volunteer work until her second child was in kindergarten.

After two years, she was juggling two part-time jobs, managing a town association and co-directing a volunteer program designed to place local high school students in work situations that matched their career interests.

She had used the nonprofit sector to acquire a wealth of business and management savvy, but she was tired of low pay. Her next move? "I wanted to climb the corporate ladder," she remembers. The first rung was a job managing sales and marketing for a company called Leisure Sports, that ran a string of very posh health clubs. But she didn't have an opportunity to climb too far before hitting a ceiling on advancement.

One nasty brush with politics left a lasting impression. On her way to her daughter's junior high school graduation one afternoon, Trish ran into resistance from her management. Because they insisted they needed her at work, she had to leave the ceremony early. "When I got back to work, they didn't even know I was back. It wasn't any big deal," she remembers. "But when I got home, my daughter was sobbing, 'Where were you? All the other parents were there.' At that point I said 'There's got to be more to life than this.'"

At about the same time, she met with a representative of Mary Kay Cosmetics to discuss conducting programs at health clubs. "I'd never heard of Mary Kay Cosmetics in my life," Trish admits. "We talked for about five minutes about the club. And then I started interviewing her. She told me she had a master's degree in finance and had moved up the banking ladder.

But working for Mary Kay Cosmetics allowed her to be independent and flexible. She made the money she wanted, yet she still had time to take her two sons to soccer and be there for them when they needed her. She could work her life around her family, instead of the other way around."

After trying the products herself, Trish decided to give it a shot. Today she is one of 225,000 independent Mary Kay beauty consultants working in 18 countries around the world.

She divides her time between her in-home studio and her clients' homes, doing one-on-one facials and teaching classes in skin care and makeup application. Although she chooses to work only 10 to 15 hours a week so that she can spend more time with her family and complete her student teaching for her degree, she has plenty of opportunity to advance.

"There's a lot of potential for anyone who is tired of the corporate rat race," Trish says. In fact, she feels proud just to be a member of a company that rewards consultants—professionally and financially—for helping fellow consultants become successful. Citing an article from *The Wall Street Journal*, she says "There are more women making more than $50,000 and more than $100,000 a year working for Mary Kay than for any other company in the world. So it's a real good business."

She encourages anyone interested in independence to investigate the opportunities. "I figure the worst that can happen is that you'll learn a lot of business and social skills that will help you in any company or any part of your life. You'll learn a lot about skin care and makeup. And you'll have a lot of fun."

## A common thread

Work as fun? That seems to be a common thread in conversations with home-based business owners. Maybe it's the times that are changing. Or maybe we are.

"Unlike the '80s, when everybody had to have more material things and everything was superficial, this is a time when everybody seems to be admiring the people who do good things for themselves," muses Donna Wotton. "The pendulum will probably swing the other way again. But by that time we'll all be established in our businesses."

# Chapter 11

# Doing your home work

You're inspired. After too many years spent stifling in the corporate world, you dream of discovering what you could achieve as your own boss. Of transforming your talent into a personal enterprise from your basement or spare bedroom. It will be tough, but you're ready. You've got some money put away, and a few clients on tap.

It will take more than that.

You believe in your talent and know you have the fire and stamina to work long hours to make your vision a reality.

It will take *still* more.

Whether you call yourself a freelancer, a contractor or a small business owner, you will need a wide range of abilities and a wealth of knowledge—beyond talent—just to survive. You'll need to know about marketing and money and how to manage your time effectively. What you don't know, you'll have to be willing to learn.

Most entrepreneurs will tell you that self-employment requires more than they ever knew they had. Having the courage to reach for your goals requires the fortitude to deal with setbacks and rejections. If you aren't ready to pay the dues or emotionally equipped to live the lifestyle day in and day out, you may find your bracing challenge is more of a rude awakening.

## A litmus test

Take a moment to answer "True" or "False" to the following questions:

**If my income were cut in half next month, I'd panic. I wouldn't be able to think about anything but my bank balance.**
      True_____   False _____

**I can't work alone for long. I have to bounce ideas off my friends, gossip, have lunch. If I couldn't do that, I'd go crazy!**
      True_____   False _____

**If I worked for myself, I'd only work three days a week and I'd never start work before noon.**
      True_____   False _____

**I'm uncomfortable talking about money. If I had to negotiate my fee, it wouldn't be worth it.**
      True_____   False _____

**I'm confident of my talents, but I'm not comfortable "selling" my abilities to others.**
      True_____   False _____

If you answered "True" to even one of these questions, you have some more homework to do.

# Part-Time Careers

If you're fresh from a layoff or chafing from years as a square peg in a round hole in the corporate environment, working at home may sound like nirvana. After all, what could be better than rolling out of bed and starting work in your bathrobe, while the rest of the world fights rush-hour traffic and corporate politics? You can spend more time with your kids. Or take a nap. Or see a movie in the middle of the afternoon. Yes, there you are on your own...all alone with a silent telephone and a dwindling bank balance.

If you've chosen to mold your part-time business to the needs of your family, you may indeed be able to work only a few days a week. But more likely, you'll have to compromise your flexibility during "feast" times—and do some pretty skillful juggling of funds to make it through the "famines." You may not have to deal with politics, but you'll become very adept at answering to the people who are your clients. Of course, you can lunch with your friends. But often you'll be bouncing your ideas off the four walls of your home office.

This isn't meant to dampen your dreams. Just wake you up to a few realities.

**Reality #1: Starting a business is risky business.** As an entrepreneur, you aren't going to let statistics dictate your life or allow yourself to be intimidated by words like "recession." That's good. But as a business person, you will have to know the whole score.

At least 65 percent of all new businesses fail within the first five years of operation. That's more than one out of every two. And many experts argue that figure is too low.

**Reality #2: Only you can make it happen.** That said, you should know that risk is a relative thing. Only you can determine how much is "manageable" for you. So take the time to do some research and some honest soul-searching. Your success will be built on two personal qualities: a hard-headed practicality about running your business and an unwavering commitment to reaching your goal.

## Five hats for one head

So, now you are the CEO. But you are also the top sales person and money changer. The slave driver and the chief bottle-washer. In short, you are in charge of everything aspect of running your business—from getting new clients to collecting the money. For each of the following roles, you'll wear a different hat.

**1. Chief financial officer.** No one is handing you a paycheck on Friday afternoon any more. So, you'll have to develop a whole new attitude about money. It is up to you set the fee for your products and services—competitive, yet adequate to meet your living expenses and overhead.

Once the money is coming in, it's up to you to make it last. Sometimes it will trickle in. At other times, it will seem to spill in. You can't be stingy when it comes to funding marketing efforts or new equipment. Yet you can't strap yourself. If you've got more work than you can handle, but no money to pay the rent, you won't be in business for long. Managing cash flow is one of your most important jobs.

"I'm billing about a third to half of what I would bill in a normal month," admits Donna Wotton. "That's a big hit when you have a payroll and bills to pay. I'm not making enough to cover my overhead. But we had a fabulous spring, so there's money in the coffers. And I've got most of the fall booked, too. So it's all going to work out. You can't panic if you have a down month. For every down month you're going to have two crazy months."

"We live very much within our means," reports Jill Hartnell. "We have a mortgage on our house, But that's our only debt. We have a lot of savings to carry us through the slow months. You just never know."

# Part-Time Careers

**2. Marketing pro.** Pounding the pavement. Cold calls. Mailings and dog-and-pony shows. Unfortunately, many of the terms used to describe the methods you'll use to reach and retain customers have a forbidding ring. But as an entrepreneur, you can't afford to resist marketing.

Your challenge—over the life of your business—will be to create a favorable impression in the minds of prospective customers—who have too much on their minds already. Not only that, you must prompt them to take action. To call you.

Your logo, business cards, stationery and brochure will establish your image, so choose them carefully. Your telephone voice will add a personal touch. But you'll have to keep in touch.

In the beginning, you may spend up to 40 percent of your time marketing your products and services to prospective customers. Here is the place to substitute money for creativity. Most entrepreneurs say the best results often come from the least expensive methods—a sample left behind, an open house, a simple black-and-white postcard. So experiment. As your business grows and changes, your tactics may also change. You'll go out of your way to keep in touch with former customers, who can often be an important source of referrals.

"I made a list of everyone I knew who had skin," says Trish Adams when she started out as a beauty consultant for Mary Kay Cosmetics. "I started with my daughter's piano teacher."

Before long, she was conducting complimentary makeovers for two women she worked with in previous jobs and another she knew through a volunteer group. "They invited some friends. Those friends had a check-up facial and invited a couple of friends, and it pretty much snowballed. Now I'm getting referrals."

"The local newspaper here has done several articles that have been seen by a very wide audience and have gotten me into other places," says Diane Hyde. In marketing her handmade jewelry and clothing, she has never relied on such lucky breaks. She experiments—and adapts what she can from other self-employed professionals.

"I do an annual Christmas show in my home. Last year I made over $2,000 in two days. Now I'm starting to think about doing some sort of an imprinted sales sheet to leave behind after sales calls and at art shows," she says.

Many entrepreneurs can benefit from joining forces with someone else in a related business. "I did a wedding cake display for a friend who is a florist," says Marie Sims. "She has my card in her shop if anyone is interested."

**3. Boss.** With no one looking over your shoulder or checking up on your progress, you're free to use your time any way you want to. You can work at night and take the afternoon off. Or sip coffee and read the newspaper all morning. Sounds great.

While it's true that you'll often have plenty of leeway in setting your work schedule, it's still up to you to complete the work on time. And sometimes you aren't given much of that. In fact, many freelancers find they have traded their boss for more relentless taskmaster—the telephone.

"I hate it when the phone rings, and I hate it when it *doesn't* ring," says Rick Kelly of his life as a freelance business writer. "If the phone's ringing all the time, you feel pressured. You have to be able live with the pressure of quick turn-arounds without going crazy—which does involve saying no now and then, and working a little too much now and then."

**4. Star performer.** For your talents and abilities to shine, you have to be goal-oriented and self-motivated. You must be able to get yourself started each day and close the door at the end of the day. You also have to pick yourself up when you're down.

"I like to do a lot of my work at night, especially when my husband is out of town on business," says Diane Hyde. "But I'm always up in the morning. It's funny, because people will call me at 9 a.m. and say, 'Are you up?' If I slept until 10, I'd never get anything done. Plus, I'd feel sloppy. I'd be angry at myself all the time for not doing anything. You have to be motivated to do anything like this. It doesn't happen unless you make it happen."

**5. Crack administrator.** You wouldn't put up with an employer who didn't give you the supplies you need to do your job, or made you work at a table in the lunchroom. So why set up your home office on the kitchen table? Your work will be challenging enough without distractions and wrestling with constant disorganization. If you don't have a talent or interest for organization, hire someone who can organize your work space for maximum efficiency. You'll be more productive—especially when you don't know what the next phone call will bring.

For Diane Hyde the next phone call often brings what she refers to as "the unknown order." When four purchase orders totaling $14,000 recently arrived by fax one evening, she was nonplused.

"It's just a logistics problem to me," she says. "I've had to learn about inventory control and producing product to meeting shipping dates. I have to work out the steps to take back in May to make a July shipping date. It's a real dance as far as buying and holding and forecasting. I have to stock up on hard-to-get items."

"When I first started out, my office was the kitchen table," remembers Donna Wotton. "I would clear it off at night and throw my work in a stack on the floor, and get it out again in the morning. Because it was in the center of the house, I always had plenty of distractions." Although she still works at home, out of a separate office on the back of her house, she has drawn a clear line between work and home life. "Now, when I close my door at 5 or 6 p.m., that's it. I pretend that this is 10 miles away from my house."

## Steps to success

If you've made it this far, you're serious about becoming your own boss. So, what now? How do you get started making your dream a reality?

**1. Test the soil.** Just because you have a great idea, or the expertise to set up shop as a copywriter doesn't necessarily mean you will be able to find enough customers to support your business. To find out if your area is fertile for your venture, you'll have to do a little investigative work.

First, check the yellow pages. If there are quite a few businesses similar to yours already listed, you might assume that the market is good. But don't jump to conclusions. Call competing business owners and ask them how business is. Find out what services they offer and what kinds of clients they serve. You might be able to specialize in some aspect of the work they don't provide. They may be willing to refer work they can't handle or clientele they can't serve to you.

In a healthy market you shouldn't have trouble getting information. If you find people are persistently close-mouthed or complain about business, it could mean there is not enough business to go around.

If there are no businesses listed similar to the one you want to start, maybe your community is ready. But to be sure, you'll have to dig further. Talk to potential customers. Discuss your plans with your local chamber of commerce and local government planning agencies. They may be able tell you about new community developments that could boost your business potential.

Read business trade and professional journals to spot emerging trends. Stay up-to-date by attending local business trade and professional meetings.

**2. Prepare a plan of action.** Using the information you've gathered, prepare a plan for your new business. It's not as intimidating as it sounds. It will be a useful tool in helping you clarify your goals and your strategies for reaching. Your business plan should have three key parts:

**Describe your business in 25 words or less.** This is the essence of your business. What is your product or service? Who will you serve? What specific benefits will you provide that make you unique among your competitors? You may want to expand this into a more detailed description you can use as a sales pitch or for a brochure.

**Write a marketing plan.** Identify your customers and describe them as thoroughly as possible. What methods will you use to reach them? How will you separate your business from the competition in their minds?

**Write a financial plan.** How much will you need to earn just to cover your living and operating expenses? How much do you want to earn? Your worksheet should also take into account the following:

- Your start-up expenses
- Your fees
- How many customers/projects you will need each month to reach your income goals.

How long will you need to supplement your income before your business can support you? A business can take anywhere from three months to over a year to turn a profit, so you should have a plan for covering your living and operating expenses during that period.

**3. Find your zone.** Most communities designate residential, commercial, industrial and agricultural zones. Even in residential areas, many zoning regulations allow for the operation of home-based businesses, although you may not be able to invite clients to your home. Check the zoning ordinances either at city hall or the county courthouse.

**4. Register.** Unless you will have a business partner or expect to run the risk of being sued for damages, you will probably begin as a sole proprietor.

The name of your business can become a valuable asset so take care to select one that is memorable, distinctive and easy to pronounce—and make sure you protect it properly. If you don't plan to use your own name, you will need to file a fictitious business name with the secretary of state or with your local county clerk, depending on your state law.

You also may wish to trademark your business name so that other people in your area can't use it.

State, county and local regulations regarding various business licenses and permits vary from place to place. Some business owners operate with only their social security number as a federal identification.

**5. Take account.** It's wise to set up a separate checking account for your business. If you don't already have a banking relationship or are looking for better service, try a small bank, where your account is more likely to be noticed and valued.

Lucky is the entrepreneur who gets money in hand at the end of a sale. "I get paid right away," says Marie Sims. She requests a deposit for each order and receives the balance on delivery. "When people are hungry, the cake is always beautiful. When they're full, they can find a lot of flaws."

Establish your terms of payment to maximize cash flow. When you can, collect at least part of the money up front in the form of a deposit or retainer. Set up a payment schedule for long projects with partial payments made at various stages of progress.

# Part-Time Careers

Instead of extending credit, take credit cards. If you must bill customers, always bill promptly and consider offering a discount of 2 to 5 percent for payments made within 10 days of the date of your invoice. Be sure to act promptly on any overdue account.

What you charge by the hour, the day, the piece or the project will be affected by your living expenses and business overhead as well as your expertise and what your market will bear.

Find out what the range is for your market. When setting your own price, stay away from either end. If you charge too much, you may lose business. If your market is competitive you may have to charge a lower price to stay in business. But don't go too low. Your customers may get the idea your services are not valuable.

"Sometimes it's just a wild guess," admits Diane Hyde of pricing her handmade jewelry. "That's the part my husband, Cam, could not grasp. He's an engineer, so he tried to do a spreadsheet with me. But being a woman, I know what women will buy. I know I'll pay a ridiculous price for some piece of jewelry that has 20 cents worth of components in it, only because I think it's beautiful. The way I put things together is what appeals to people. So the price should reflect that uniqueness."

She begins by calculating the cost of the components and the time involved in assembling each piece of jewelry she designs. "Now that I have $7 total materials and time invested, I ask myself, 'What is it worth to someone at an art show or in a department store?' I compare it to other pieces that I sell—the high end and low end. I'm still amazed at what people will pay at art shows for an item."

Keep careful track of what you earn and what you spend. There are a lot of books that can help you set up a reliable bookkeeping and accounting system for your business and a number of software products that help you track tax-deductible items and generate reports, such as monthly profit and loss. The better your records, the more prepared you'll be if you are audited. If you're uncomfortable with any aspect of your financial recordkeeping, by all means hire an accountant who specializes in home-based business.

As soon as you start your own business, whether full-time or part-time, convert some of your costs of living into tax-deductible business expenses. If you're still working, change the number of allowances you claim on your W-4 withholding form so that you add as many additional dollars to your take-home pay as you can. You can use the extra money to fund your start-up and write it off on your next tax return.

**6. Step into your office.** To guard against interruptions, as well as against working around the clock, set up your home office in a spare bedroom, basement or, at the very least, in an area that is partitioned off from the rest of your living space. Install a separate telephone line. If you can only afford the minimum equipment and furnishings, look for used items. But don't scrimp on your comfort or your professionalism.

**7. Identify yourself.** Spend time with a designer discussing the type of logo and graphic image you want to convey through your stationery and business cards. If you can't afford to pay much for design, hire a college student or arrange to barter your services with a professional designer.

Because some of your clients may know you only through your stationery, it's important to make sure that your graphic image is consistent with your business persona. If you are a computer consultant, for example, you'll want to convey a modern, high-tech image—one that would be inappropriate for a day-care provider.

A graphic designer long before she began her jewelry business, Diane Hyde designed her own logo, with excellent results. "I found that the recognition factor was astounding," she says. "I've already established a 'visual' following in a few short years." Her first name followed by a swashy "H" makes an impression because it's pleasing and conveys quality.

**8. Set your hours.** You may find there is not a "typical" day. And of course, as the boss, you are free to work when—and if—you want. But most home-based entrepreneurs find it helpful to set a basic work schedule. Family members will know when not to disturb you and you won't be as likely to let work take over your life.

"If I call my friends, I say 'Hi, let me tell you about a new product we have available.' I deal with business immediately and then I'll chat," says Trish Adams. "If someone starts chatting, I let them know that I have to make 20 calls in an hour, so I only have a couple of minutes. But I promise to give them a call when I'm through. I let them know that this is serious business."

## Tips from the experts

From learning how to delegate to knowing when to "play hooky," you'll find your own way to cope with the stresses and rewards of being a home-based business owner. Here's some advice to get you started.

**Do what you know.** And something you do well. If you're lacking skill or expertise in some area, sign up for training and practice your skills on family members before your try them out on prospective customers. A poor or mediocre job is the best way to turn away potential customers. Some customers refuse to pay for inferior work. With a solid experience and professional contacts you'll be able to move ahead confidently.

**Learn what you need to know.** If you're an entrepreneur, you'll never stop learn. So read books and keep up with trade journals. Take seminars.

"Up until now, we've both been pretty specific about what we do," says Jill Hartnell. "I've focused on all the accounts payable projects and Kevin has focused on all the general ledger projects." But that changed when they made a mutual decision to take on an accounts payable project with a very tight deadline. Since the only way they could complete the work was to share it, "Kevin is starting to learn some of the things that I do," says Jill.

"If you want to freelance at something, learn the craft by working for a company first. You get paid for learning it. When you leave, you'll have contacts and credentials and a track record," advises Rick Kelly. But even after he was on his own, he kept his ears open. "I've had to sit and develop strategy with marketing directors of companies and with high-level marketing people in agencies. Over the course of 10 or 12 years of doing this I'm probably as good at a lot of aspects of high strategy and marketing as people who've just gotten their MBAs. By this point I have something to contribute in terms of what pieces work for what audiences, what you want to say to what people."

**Treat the client as the boss.** "Some people have rules. They'll say, 'I won't do it unless I have three weeks' notice,' " says Marie. "If I have time and I can squeeze it in, why not?"

"In my business, out of sight is out of mind," says Rick Kelly. "I'm finding it hard to just say no as a freelancer. Most clients have to proceed on a certain schedule. If they have to form a relationship with another supplier and it's good, they will be very reluctant to interrupt it to resume what was formerly a good relationship."

**Know when to say *when*.** "I tried to set up a trunk show in San Francisco during our last trip out and I decided, 'Hey, I'm tired. This is a vacation,' " admits Diane Hyde. "The logistics came into the picture. I realized, 'I've got to take inventory. I've got to take all my tools, my components. This is not going to be fun. So I thought, 'Do I need it? Or do I need a vacation?' So I didn't pursue it."

**Play hooky from time to time.** "I used to have a friend who owned an advertising agency, a complete manic workaholic," says Donna Wotton. "She used to pay me to plan a surprise outing for her entire staff on a work day once a month. We went river rafting or took a big picnic lunch somewhere. It usually involved fresh air and no work. The following day they could worry about whatever deadline they missed."

**Build a network.** Some networks are built in. Others you must forge on your own. Some are set up for business purposes, others for support. Both kinds are crucial to the survival and emotional well-being of home-based business owners.

At Mary Kay Cosmetics, the corporate structure seems fashioned for networking. "It's the only company I've ever heard of where you go up to someone and say 'I'd like your job,' and they say, 'Great, I'll help you.' And they do," marvels Trish Adams. "We have unit meetings every week. I also get together weekly with several consultants to talk business over coffee. There are no secrets. If somebody finds something that works for them, they can't wait to pass it on the someone else."

**When the going gets tough, have faith.** "One day you have all these deals coming through and you get so excited. And the next day, well this one fell through for that reason and that one fell through for this reason and you're asking yourself 'What did I do wrong? What could I have done better?' " says Jill Hartnell. "It's hard to take the hits and keep on going. But if you lose your confidence in yourself, you're not going to be able to sell yourself—and you may not be able to do the best job possible."

"Women haven't traditionally been conditioned to handle rejection," says Trish Adams. "So when we get into a position where we have to ask for things, sometimes we get a no. I think it's hard for some people to accept the rejection at first. Through Mary Kay Cosmetics, we're taught constantly that they're not rejecting you, they're rejecting the offer. One woman says she just smiles and says 'Thank you'—but in the back of her mind she's thinking, 'OK, go wrinkle!'"

**Delegate...very carefully.** "I had a rep working for me for a while," says Diane Hyde. "She got me into some really nice places. But sometimes she sold too much. I was scrambling to make orders, because they'd order one of these and one of those. It's easier to make 10 of these and 10 of those."

But when it comes to delegating tasks within her business, she finds her biggest problem has been just letting go. "That has been pure ego," she admits. "My biggest fear is losing quality. I don't want pieces coming back to me because the jump rings came open. I've always been a stickler for making sure everything is done just so before it leaves my hands. I have to find the right people who can do that for me.

It's not always easy to share the load with someone else. "When I get very busy, people ask me why I don't hire someone or work with someone," says Rick Kelly. "My clients want me to write something based on what they see of my portfolio. A lot of clients would be very upset if they found that I was farming the work out to someone."

**Have a plan and, when in doubt, reassess.** "Once a year, my husband and I sit down with an easel and chart and talk about everything in regard to the business," says Diane Hyde. "I have the luxury of knowing the industry. Cam takes it from there. He helps me see things that I don't see in the creative swirl that's going on above my head. Creative people tend to be sort of 'La, la, la... Everything's beautiful and it'll happen. And it'll be easy, right?' But it's not."

But don't wait for once a year. "In the past month, I told him, 'I get so lethargic in regard to my direction and my jewelry. It's almost like I've lost interest.' He said 'No, it's just time to reassess your goals.' A light went on. I have been wanting to pursue screenprinting for the past year. That's when I decided to pursue it."

**Fit your work into your life.** "I probably work my Mary Kay business 10 to 15 hours a week. That's about all it takes," says Trish Adams. "I make stars on my calendar at the times I want to be available. That way I make sure that I work around my family. For example, Friday night is 'date night.' If somebody asks for a Friday night appointment, I say, 'I'm sorry, I have a date.'"

**Fit a *life* into your work.** "Part of the reason I'm not working a 9-to-5 job is so I don't have to *be* 9-to-5. You can create your own structure if you work for yourself," says Rick Kelly. But he admits, "That's the blessing and the curse. Sometimes it's difficult for me to make a personal appointment two weeks in advance. If I'm waiting to get feedback on a project and Thursday isn't that busy, I don't mind working on Sunday. But you can end up working all the time, or all the hours when everybody else is free.

"If I had a family, I couldn't get away with this. I think I'd have to structure my time differently so I had more time for my family and so things were more consistent."

**Do it because you love it.** "If you're just being self-employed because you don't have a job right now, find another job, or enjoy your leisure time," advises Donna Wotton. "You have to do it for good reasons."

# Chapter 12

# Home-based businesses: 10 best for the '90s

Whether you're interested in developing a hobby into a money-making endeavor, carving out a reputation in your field of expertise or simply want to spend more time with your family, you can find a home-based business suited to your goals and lifestyle.

The important thing is to choose something you really enjoy doing and that will give you the income you require. As you evaluate the businesses listed here—or other viable businesses—ask yourself these questions:

**1. What kind of lifestyle do I want?** How much time will I have to spend working? How flexible is my schedule likely to be? Will seasonal or weekend work be required? Will I have to travel a lot of the time? Spend a lot of my time working alone?

"Do what's compatible with the rest of your life," advises Donna Wotton. "Do it because you truly enjoy it, because it's fun, because you want to do it every day." If you don't find a business that appeals to you here, you'll find the same detail on 70 home businesses in *Best Home Businesses for the '90s,* by Paul and Sarah Edwards.

**2. How much can I earn?** How much will I need to earn to cover my living expenses and business overhead? How much do I want to earn? What are the start-up costs, and how soon can I expect to see a return on my investment? How much money will I need to invest in equipment, wardrobe, marketing and promotion?

Each of the businesses listed here offers good potential for a comfortable, steady income. But what is comfortable for another person may not be adequate for you. Don't underestimate the importance of money in your quality of life. By the same token, don't overestimate it. Choosing a home-based career is often a matter of striking a balance between lifestyle and monetary rewards.

## How to read the trends

Take a moment to review the broad rendering of trends in demographics, business and lifestyle in Chapter 4. They may also signal the types of home-based businesses that are likely to prosper through the coming decade,

It makes sense, for example, that service businesses—such as residential cleaning and day-care—will be in demand when you consider the rising number of two-income households. But sometimes the connection between trends and opportunity is not so clear. Pay attention to jobs that seem to be disappearing from the corporate arena. Many, such as meeting planning and corporate training, are being reborn at home.

Most of the following businesses already have a track record for success. Even if your prospective business is not listed here, use the criteria on the next page as a guideline for selecting your own business that is right for you.

**Knowledge and skills required.** Every business demands certain talents and aptitudes. Some businesses require a license and special training. Use this information as a guide to the requirements you'll need to run each business.

**Start-up costs.** How much will it take to get the business going? A cleaning service may be started with as little as a few hundred dollars. A desktop publishing venture that depends on sophisticated computer technology may require an initial investment of as much as $10,000.

The low end of the range listed for each business will give you the estimated cost for:

- **A minimally equipped office.** That is, a standard four-drawer filing cabinet, desk, comfortable chair, standard IBM-compatible computer, dot-matrix printer and printer stand. You may be able to buy used equipment or postpone buying more costly equipment by leasing it.

- **A logo, business cards, stationery and a brochure.** Don't scrimp on design or paper quality. With a laser printer, you can produce custom brochures using a variety of colored and textured papers.

  While additional marketing costs are not included in this start-up figure, you should factor it in to ensure your success of your business.

- **Dues for professional or trade organizations.** Your best avenue for building business is through regularly networking with prospective customers and your professional peers.

- **Supplies and accessories.** The basic tools of the trade will vary by business—from paper and pens for a copywriter to the toys and cribs a day-care provider will need to the shrink-wrap machine the owner of a gift-basket business can't live without.

The fancier your office, the slicker your brochures, the more sophisticated your computer, the higher your start-up costs will be. Look to the top end of the range.

**Advantages/disadvantages.** If you hate to work under pressure of deadlines, don't consider copywriting. If you value your freedom of movement, don't start a day-care business. This straight talk can help you avoid investing in a business you are likely to abandon later on.

**What to charge/potential earnings.** The rates you can charge—whether by the hour, the day, the project or the piece—will depend on many factors. The geographical area you live in, the type of clients you serve, your reputation and experience all affect your earning. The rates listed here reflect typical earnings in urban areas.

Annual gross revenues are based on what you could earn billing 20 hours per week. Most freelancers use the other 20 hours to handle paperwork, marketing and other business-related tasks.

**How to get business.** You can expect to be marketing your business over the life of your business. These are just a few methods for getting the word out to prospective customers.

**How to get started.** Taking that first step can be intimidating. Here are some tips on how to begin.

**Where to get help.** Professional associations are wonderful resources for books, seminars, accredited training programs and other information that will help you get started and maintain your expertise over the life of your business.

# 10 of the Best

## 1. Cleaning Service

Home cleaning is a $92 million dollar industry, making it one of the fastest-growing segments of the economy. It is also among the easiest businesses to start profitably from your home. In addition, there are a growing number of cleaning franchises and training and licensing programs.

**Knowledge and skills required.** Other than a willingness to work hard, you'll need very little formal knowledge or experience. You can get free technical expertise from janitorial supply houses and product manufacturers.

**Start-up costs.** You can start a residential cleaning service with an investment of $1,000 in basic professional supplies and cleaning equipment. Overhead costs are low.

**Advantages.** Cleaning is an ongoing need, so you should find it easy to build a repeat clientele. By adding crews of workers, you can expand your business even more—and still run it from home.

**Disadvantages.** You'll have to overcome a low status image. Cleaning is hard and dirty work. Some types of cleaning are seasonal and periodic. Unless you have employees, your income is limited by the number of hours you can work in a day.

**What to charge/potential earnings.** Fees generally run from $50 to $75 a day, or $10 to $20 an hour. Annual income can range from $20,000 to $30,000 a year.

**How to get business.** Advertise in community newspapers and the local yellow pages. Distribute fliers in neighborhoods or post them in coin laundries or grocery stores. Offer new customers introductory discounts. Keep in touch with customers who use your services periodically.

**How to get started.** Rent, rather than buy equipment you plan to use infrequently. Offer to help out other services on days when you aren't working.

Contact one of the many franchises that can help you get started in business, such as Classy Maids, Box 160879, Altamonte Springs, FL 32716-0879. 1 (800) 445-5238.

**Where to get help.** Call or write for a copy of the book, *Everything You Need to Know to Start a Housecleaning Service,* by Mary Pat Johnson, Cleaning Consultant Services, Box 1273, Seattle, WA 98111. (206) 682-9748.

## 2. Computer Consultant

Acting as hardware and software experts, programmers and technical and business advisers, computer consultants take a broad view of the computer needs within a business, organization or department. They work closely with a variety of people—from managers to computer users—to install and upgrade equipment or software, conduct training and solve a variety of business problems.

**Knowledge and skills required.** In addition to up-to-date technical knowledge of hardware and software, consultants must understand how a business or department works. They must be resourceful and able to communicate with a variety of people. Consultants who specialize in one area, such as financial systems, should have an overall understanding of the procedures and requirements of the field, so they can provide comprehensive solutions.

**Start-up costs.** Because computer consultants need to have access to equipment as advanced as the computer systems their clients use, start-up costs can range from $6,000 to $15,000.

**Advantages.** The outlook is bright for computer consultants. The work is varied and the hours flexible. Some travel may be required, although many computer consultants can work from anywhere in the country.

**Disadvantages.** In addition to the pressure of deadlines, consultants must spend a great deal of time staying up-to-date on changes in the computer field. Often, it is difficult to estimate project costs.

**What to charge/potential earnings.** Depending on the type of clients, market, degree of specialization, industry and types of projects they handle, computer consultants may earn $25 to $135 an hour. Gross annual revenues range from $45,000 to $300,000.

**How to get business.** Potential clients can be found at computer and software user group meetings, through on-line computer services and bulletin board systems, and in trade and business associations serving specialized industries. Consultants can benefit by joining or forming business referral groups and gain visibility by speaking at civic, trade and professional organizations, teaching courses in colleges, conducting seminars at conferences and trade shows and writing articles for trade publications. Many consultants begin by working for their former employers. Some act as distributors of quality hardware or software products.

**How to get started.** After gaining experience by working as an internal consultant, it's wise to start with a contract large enough to cover your overhead and living expenses for an extended period.

**Where to get help.** Write or call the Independent Computer Consultants Association, 933 Gardenview Office Parkway, St. Louis, MO 63141. 1 (800) GET-ICCA.

## 3. Copywriter

Copywriters know how to crystallize the key benefits of a product or service using clear, concise descriptions and call-to-action writing. Freelance copywriters help a variety of businesses—from local health clubs to major corporations—capture the attention of prospective customers and motivate them to buy. They may work on a range of materials, including advertisements, direct-mail brochures, instruction manuals, grant proposals, media kits, feature stories, annual reports and video scripts.

**Knowledge and skills required.** Although no special background is required, copywriters must be able to synthesize

# Part-Time Careers

sometimes complex information into a clear, interesting, compelling message. Imagination and curiosity help them take a fresh approach to describe a product and service.

**Start-up costs.** Costs range from $2,550 to $6,000. In addition to a computer with a hard-disk drive, copywriters need word-processing software and a range of reference books. Some writers invest in on-line reference sources such as Prodigy or CD-ROM software.

**Advantages.** Most copywriters are able to fix their own hours. They have the satisfaction of holding the finished product in their hand at the completion of a project.

**Disadvantages.** Often copywriters work under the pressure of tight deadlines. The work may be difficult if a subject matter is complex, highly technical or unfamiliar to the writer.

**What to charge/potential earnings.** Hourly fees range from $30 to $150, with the average about $70. Day rates for consulting on a direct-mail project range from $1,500 to $2,000. Fees for projects, such as direct-mail packages, range from $2,000 to $7,000.

Annual revenues range from $20,000 in the first year up to $175,000 for professionals with five years or more experience.

**How to get business.** Let everyone you meet know that you are a writer. Show them your portfolio, containing samples of your work. Become active in trade and business associations, particularly in industries or fields in which you have experience. Develop affiliations with related professionals, such as graphic designers, photographers and printers, who can refer work to you.

**How to get started.** Create a portfolio with at least five samples of your writing to show clients. Take business and writing courses offered by local writers' groups, extension programs, colleges and universities.

**Where to get help.** Write or call the International Association of Business Communicators, 1 Hallidie Plaza, Suite 600, San Francisco, CA 94102. (415) 433-3400.

## 4. Corporate Trainer

Ongoing training will become a fact of life for most workers in the '90s. The American Society for Training and Development (ASTD) estimates that 50 million people—42 percent of the work force—will need additional training in technical skills, management, customer service—even basic literacy.

While many large organizations have supported in-house staffs in the past, more and more are turning to outside trainers who specialize in one or more areas.

**Knowledge and skills required.** In addition to skill or expertise, trainers need to be able to present information effectively to a wide spectrum of audiences. Good organizational and writing skills are necessary in preparing proposals and course materials. Good interpersonal skills help trainers inspire students during the learning process and sell their programs to management decision-makers.

**Start-up costs.** Costs range from $3,500 to $10,000. To produce training materials, trainers might need a computer with a hard disk, laser printer, word-processing software with desktop publishing capabilities and a comb binding machine to bind workbooks.

**Advantages.** Training is intellectually stimulating and rewarding. Many trainers are born performers and are comfortable being "on stage" frequently. Some develop books, tapes and other products related to their "live" programs to provide an ongoing income.

**Disadvantages.** Because many of the benefits of training are intangible, it is a "product" that is often difficult to sell. Trainers may spend up to 80 percent of their time selling their services. Frequent travel may be necessary.

**What to charge/potential earnings.** Most corporate trainers charge a day rate ranging from $600 to $2,000. Some charge $100 or more per trainee. Annual revenue can range from $31,000 to $230,000. Trainers who work three days a week at $600 a day will gross $75,600 per year.

**How to get business.** Demonstrate what you can do by speaking before professional and trade associations. Directly solicit potential clients using a combination of phone contacts, customized mailings and personal appointments. Write articles for trade and professional journals.

**How to get started.** Although you don't need formal training to become a corporate trainer, it is wise to stick to an industry in which you've already developed expertise. If necessary, take a course in selling or consult an image consultant to enhance your presentation skills. For each program you plan to market, develop a step-by-step course outline that tells what you intend to teach and what specific skills and knowledge trainees can expect to gain. Test your training program on volunteers at nonprofit organizations.

**Where to get help.** Write or call the American Society for Training Development, 1630 Duke St., Alexandria, VA 22313. (703) 683-8100.

## 5. Day-care Provider

Today 57 percent of all married women and 70 percent of divorced women with children under the age of six years work outside the home. In addition, 50 percent of women who work at home use some form of childcare at least part of the time.

Yet families complain that good day-care is hard to come by. There's little question that quality day-care providers will be in demand throughout the '90s.

**Knowledge and skills required.** Day-care providers caring for one or more children in their homes should enjoy children and understand their behavior and development. They should be upbeat and patient, as well as tactful and tolerant of parents. Often it is necessary to organize four or five activities at a time. Many former teachers adjust very well as home-based day-care providers.

About one in four home-based operators is licensed. Licensing is necessary to receive food subsidies and liability insurance. To be licensed, a day-care provider must have adequate space for children to play in the home and yard, as well as ample toys for them to play with. Cleaning supplies and other dangerous household chemicals must be locked safely away.

**Start-up costs.** Costs range from $2,500 to $3,700. Day-care providers need to have adequate liability insurance as well as toys, beds and cribs or playpens, safety equipment, such as fire extinguishers, and a cordless telephone.

**Advantages.** Day-care providers can earn a living while they stay at home with their own children. It is possible to deduct rooms used for childcare on state and federal tax returns, even if those rooms are used for nonbusiness purposes at other times.

**Disadvantages.** Day-care providers are confined to their homes and yards for approximately 10 hours every weekday. For long periods, their contact is limited to small children.

**What to charge/potential earnings.** Providers earn from $38 to $118 per child per week, with a median income of $75 per child per week. Annual revenues can be $23,400, plus $6,240 in Child Care Food Program funds, for six children at $75 per child per week.

**How to get business.** List your services as a day-care provider with a referral agency. Network with other family day-care providers so that you can take on their overflow business. Post fliers on bulletin boards in coin laundries, community centers and churches. Advertise in local newspapers.

**How to get started.** Check zoning requirements in your area and talk with neighbors about your plans. Contact a childcare information agency or a family day-care association to assess the demand in your area, learn about licensing requirements and find sources for training. Establish rates and policies, including hours of operation, deposits, late fees, holidays, notice of termination and payment. Obtain necessary equipment and child-proof your home.

**Where to get help.** Write or call the National Association for Family DayCare, 725 15th St. N.W., Suite 505, Washington, D.C. 20005. 1 (800) 359-3817.

# 6. Desktop Publishing Service

Sophisticated computer technology and desktop publishing software programs have eliminated many of the time-consuming and

# Part-Time Careers

costly steps in preparing printed materials, such as typesetting and paste-up. So, an increasing number of businesses can afford to produce a variety of internal and external communications, such as newsletters and directories. Some desktop publishers run a booming business from home, while others may temporarily work on-site for companies.

**Knowledge and skills required.** In addition to computer skills and an extensive knowledge of desktop publishing software, desktop publishers must be able to write clearly and have a working knowledge of the elements of good design as well as of printing practices and procedures. Interpersonal skills are also essential, especially for desktop publishers working with clients who are novices in design and print production.

**Start-up costs.** Costs range from $7,600 to $20,000. Most desktop publishers need a Macintosh or IBM-compatible computer with a large hard disk and full-page monitor. Desktop publishers also need a high-quality laser printer and appropriate software and type fonts.

**Advantages.** The work is interesting and creative. Desktop publishers have ample opportunity to develop new skills. Because the field is growing rapidly, the potential for income is good.

**Disadvantages.** The field is becoming increasingly competitive. In addition to facing deadline pressures, desktop publishers must stay up-to-date on the latest advances in software.

**What to charge/potential earnings.** Hourly rates range from $25 to $65. Per-page rates range from $25 to $50. Many clients prefer to pay one fixed price for a project, so desktop publishers must be adept at estimating the number of hours a job will take, allowing for corrections and changes.

Annual revenues average about $40,000, based on four billable hours a day at $40 per hour. By offering additional services, such as pickup and delivery, fast turnaround and high-quality printing, desktop publishers can increase their income.

**How to get business.** Arrange to show your portfolio to print shops, small service and retail businesses, professional practices and nonprofit organizations. Network at organizations. Advertise in the yellow pages or send direct-mail promotions to specific markets in large metropolitan areas. Offer new clients a discount on their first order—one hour free with a minimum four-hour job, for example. Watch for want ads placed by companies seeking graphic design personnel to handle overflow work.

**How to get started.** If you don't have experience in graphic design, sign up for a course through a continuing education program, or at a local college or art school. Learn about service bureaus and printers. Find a specialty market that hasn't been tapped by other desktop publishers.

**Where to get help.** Write or call the National Association of Desktop Publishers, Box 1410, Boston, MA 02215. (617) 426- 2885.

## 7. Executive Recruiter

Call it "headhunting" or "matchmaking." Executive recruiters are paid by employers to find qualified people to fill management, professional and technical jobs in a wide variety of industries. Because the overwhelming amount of work is done on the telephone, 25 percent of the 28,000 recruitment firms are home-based businesses with one or two employees. Many successful recruiters specialize in placing a certain type of personnel in a certain industry.

**Knowledge and skills required.** In addition to knowing the trends and types of people needed in a specialized industry, executive recruiters must be good at judging character. In developing relationships between companies and prospective recruits, they must be patient and tenacious.

**Start-up costs.** Costs range from $3,500 to $9,500. Most recruiters need a computer with a hard disk, an ink-jet or laser printer, modem and fax machine. They also need database, word-processing and communications software. Many invest in a telephone headset.

**Advantages.** Start-up costs are low, while potential income can be very high.

**Disadvantages.** Because executive recruiters are paid only when they make a successful "match," the business can be risky. The closure rate for executive searches is about half. Big wins and losses can be stressful. Recruiters must have the self-confidence and motivation to make plenty of cold calls.

**What to charge/potential earnings.** Executive recruiters charge from 20 to 40 percent of the first year's earnings of the professionals they place. Some work on contingency. Some work on a retainer, collecting 30 percent of their total fee upon acceptance of the search, 30 percent within 30 days and 30 percent at the end of 60 days.

Annual revenues averaged $122,000 in 1990. Most recruiters complete 15 searches per year.

**How to get business.** Call companies that have repeatedly advertised for a particular position in trade and professional publications. Write a script for your telephone calls and use it over and over. Make contacts at trade shows. Speak about recruitment to professional and trade associations. Mail postcards advertising your business to prospective companies.

**How to get started.** Go to work for an existing firm where you can learn about a specific industry.

**Where to get help.** Write or call the Association of Executive Search Consultants, 151 Railroad Avenue, Greenwich, CT 06830. (203) 661-6010.

## 8. Facialist

By the year 2000, more than half the population will be over the age of 35. The services facialists can provide men and women will be increasingly in demand. People in all occupations—from executives to flight attendants—who want to continue to put their best face forward will turn to facialists.

Facialists help clients of all ages take care of their skin, using cleansing products and routines to avert wrinkles and skin problems and generally slow down the natural process of aging. Many sell skin care products, as well.

**Knowledge and skills required.** Most facialists complete training and are licensed as cosmeticians. To be successful, they must combine an outgoing personality with a nurturing nature. Facialists should be comfortable touching and maintaining close physical contact with their clients.

**Start-up costs.** Costs range from $7,200 to $13,200, not including remodeling or decorating a home studio. Most facialists need a table, steamer, sterilizer and other special equipment.

**Advantages.** The work is not stressful or physically demanding. Potential income often depends on developing a steady, repeat clientele. Facialists can see clients during the hours they choose.

**Disadvantages.** To see clients in their home, facialists must equip and decorate a separate room as a salon. In some areas, zoning restrictions may become an issue.

**What to charge/potential earnings.** Most facialists charge by the appointment. A basic facial runs between $35 and $60, with $45 as the average.

**How to get business.** Tell your personal contacts about your business. Pass out product catalogues to friends. Create a "beauty adviser" newsletter to send to past and prospective clients. Offer special rates or complimentary facials via postcards or fliers. Sell gift certificates or hold an open house at which you provide information about your services.

**How to get started.** Complete a six-month training program to become a professional cosmetician through a private school or community college. Set up a room in your home as a salon and begin marketing your services.

There are a number of franchises that can help you get started as a professional beauty consultant, such as Mary Kay Cosmetics, 8787 Stemmons Freeway, Dallas, TX 75247. (214) 630-8787.

**Where to get help.** Write or call the National Association of Aestheticians, 3606 Prescott, Dallas, TX 75219. (214) 526-0760.

## 9. Gift Basket Business

In a hectic and often impersonal world, giving a customized gift—that takes no time to select, wrap and deliver—can speak volumes at any time of year. Gift baskets are perfect for birthdays and other special occasions, as well as for business gifts.

In fact, the most profitable market is the corporate market. But gift baskets are also increasingly popular with wedding planners, resort hotels, meeting planners, contest operators and so on. Some people create baskets for special markets, such as hospital patients. With enough ingenuity and some marketing savvy, this can develop into a profitable part-time or full-time business.

**Knowledge and skills required.** Imagination and an artistic flair are essential in this business. But gift basket creators also need plenty of business savvy. They must know where to purchase supplies cost-effectively and be able to manage their time and inventory to operate efficiently during peak seasons.

**Start-up costs.** Costs range from $2,300 to $11,000. Gift baskets are built from an initial inventory of food and other items. A hot-glue gun, shrink-wrap machine and professional portfolio with photographs of finished baskets are also essential.

**Advantages.** You can earn a living by using creative expression. This is an easy business to start on a part-time basis.

**Disadvantages.** Business tends to be seasonal. Holidays are especially hectic so it helps to have a partner or assistant. Inventory and production can take up a lot space. Larger mail-order gift basket companies can offer tough competition.

**What to charge/potential earnings.** Depending on its size, the time it takes to assemble and its artistic quality, a gift basket may be priced anywhere from $10 to $300. Most sell for between $35 and $50.

Selling 25 baskets a week, 50 weeks a year at $40 a basket will produce $50,000 in gross sales. The cost of components should be about 25 percent of the selling price.

**How to get business.** Assemble a portfolio of your work and show it to prospective buyers in corporations and organizations. Leave a simple basket behind. Provide a gift basket as a door prize at meetings. Display your baskets at home parties and open houses and take orders. Give your fliers and brochures to representatives at gift shows.

**How to get started.** If you have no experience in design, take a course in floral design through your community college or a university extension program. Locate sources of supplies at trade shows and through wholesalers. Obtain MasterCard and Visa merchant accounts.

**Where to get help.** Write or call to receive a copy of the "Gift Basket Service Business Guide," *Entrepreneur Magazine*, 2392 Morse Avenue, Box 19787, Irvine, CA 92713. 1 (800) 421-2300. In California, 1 (800) 352-7449.

# 10. Meeting/Event Planner

From private parties to major conventions, meeting/event planners handle all the details—from planning the budget to developing presentations. Corporations, associations and nonprofit organizations regularly use meeting/event planners to pull together complex arrangements for conventions, fund-raising events, banquets, hospitality events and sales meetings.

**Knowledge and skills required.** Resourcefulness, excellent organizational skills and grace under pressure are essential. Meeting/event planners must enjoy working with a wide range of people.

**Start-up costs.** Costs range from $2,500 to $6,500. Most meeting/event planners need a computer with a hard disk, word-processing and database software, an inkjet or laser printer and a fax machine. Many use a telephone headset and cellular telephone.

**Advantages.** Meeting/event planners are not only well-compensated, but they often are invited to participate in the events they plan—from informal bashes to champagne-and-caviar events.

# Part-Time Careers

**Disadvantages.** Crisis can be the norm. Meeting/event planners must be ready for the unexpected, such as a blizzard that closes an airport, or a hotel that mixes up reservations.

**What to charge/potential earnings.** Meeting/events planners may charge an hourly rate, a flat fee or a percentage of the total budget. Annual revenues range from $25,000 to $100,000.

**How to get business.** Meet other planners at local chapter meetings of Meeting Planners International. Cultivate contacts among local banquet and catering managers. Volunteer to plan a charity or civic event to demonstrate your capabilities, make contacts and get referrals. Subscribe to calendars published by your city convention bureaus to learn of upcoming meetings and events.

**How to get started.** Write or call for a copy of the *Entrepreneur Magazine* "Event Planning Business Guide," 2392 Morse Avenue, Box 19787, Irvine, CA 92713. 1 (800) 421-2300.

**Where to get help.** Write or call Meeting Planners International 1950 Stemmons Freeway, Dallas, TX 75207. (214) 746-5224.

# "Gotta dance:" Using part-time work to pursue a passion

*"There is only one success—to be able to spend your life in your own way."*
—Christopher Morley

# Chapter 13

# Working to live—so you can live to work

Gotta dance? Or sing? Or write? Whatever your dream, it has become your life's passion. It drives you and delights you. It wakes you up in the middle of the night. It is your most consuming challenge, and sometimes your greatest curse. Yet, you can't conceive of living your life any other way.

To those who don't share your commitment, your single-minded insistence to do "whatever it takes" to achieve your goals may be laudable—but incomprehensible. The uncertain path you've chosen, the sacrifices you make, may appear foolhardy.

For you, there couldn't be anything more certain than trusting the talent or hobby or business that now seems to have taken on a life of its own, and is leading you in the direction of your dreams. Whatever sacrifices you have to make along the way seem inconsequential.

Part-time work allows you to support a pursuit that may not now—may not ever—fully support you. But what starts out as a means to an end often takes on a richness and meaning of its own. Even work in an unrelated field can begin to nourish another, very distinct side of yourself.

How do you arrive at this life? Maybe you've always been certain of the passion that will shape your life. Or friends first prodded you to see the possibilities of this tough road you've chosen. Maybe your purpose whispered in your ear more than once, becoming more insistent until you finally understood.

As the following people confirm, it doesn't matter how your life's passion finds you. Once it does, you know it. And there is no turning back.

## 'Stuck with it'

Her first brush with destiny came early in her college career when she wrote a short fiction story for an English class. "It came to me in one fell swoop," remembers Tracy Fetters. "I wrote it in one sitting, like I was taking dictation." But when her instructor encouraged her to pursue a career as a fiction writer, she ignored his advice.

"I was always told you couldn't make a living as a fiction writer," she says. "Besides, I had my blinders on to be a lawyer. I had always planned on going to law school."

What she couldn't ignore was that law school just didn't feel right. After struggling part-way through her third year, Tracy decided to drop out, move across the country to San Francisco and work as a bartender for a while "to clear my mind." Then, she was riding the bus to work one day and fate tapped her again.

"I got this very well-defined idea for a long story," she remembers. "When I got to work, I sat in the back of the restaurant and wrote out the short version of the plot as it came to me, with the names of the main characters. It was clear that this was a novel. I thought, 'Great. I have novel in my head. I don't have time to write a novel. I don't even know how. Forget it!' "

So instead, she concentrated on parlaying her first freelance writing project into a career as a freelance business and legal writer and editor.

# Part-Time Careers

But the novel in her head refused to leave her alone. "For several years, I would wake up in the middle of the night with my characters talking to each other, and I'd write down major scenes," she says. "I thought 'I'm stuck with this. It's not a question of disciplining myself to sit down and write now. If anything, I have to discipline myself *not* to think about it so I can work and make a living.'"

The turning point came when she enrolled in a correspondence workshop for budding novelists and wrote the first 50 pages of her novel. She realized, "Not only can I write this novel, but I'm going to write more novels." It wasn't long before she traded the uncertain schedule and income of her freelance writing business for the stability of a part-time job as an editor for a publishing company. "Working five or six hours a day, I could come home and write for the rest of the day. That way, I was able to finish the first third of the first draft."

Now halfway through the first draft of her novel, Tracy dreams of the day when she may be able to support herself by writing fiction. "I'm very realistic about that. I don't believe this book or the books I would write in the future will be commercial. So I'd be satisfied writing novels half or three-quarters of my time and continuing writing or editing nonfiction, like I'm doing now, to supplement that. I still love working with words."

She is matter-of-fact about the obstacles she's encountered. They have only fired her drive to finally reach her goal. "There have been times when I've had to go back to working full-time for a while just to make ends meet. At those times, I didn't have the time or creative energy to work on my book. The effect of that has been very significant. It feels like I'm drowning in my inability to let this out."

For her, there is one bottom line. "Even though it may make you suffer in other areas of your life, it's wonderful to be absolutely in love with what you do."

## Bringing up baby

Like a series of snapshots, the stages of Eleanor Bissell's life tell the story of a career as a freelance photographer that, according to her, "just evolved."

While working full-time as a psychiatric nurse, Eleanor noticed that many of the psychotic children in her care were drawn to photographs of themselves. Rescuing her camera from her closet at home, she started documenting their daily lives, eventually creating picture books for individual children around a theme that was as unique as they were.

Meanwhile, members of the hospital staff were noticing her skill in capturing candid expressions and began asking her to photograph their weddings and children. "I had never defined myself as a photographer. I had always just taken pictures of myself and my family," she says. She agreed to photograph her first two weddings with the disclaimer: "I won't know how to pose you if you ask. If I get group pictures, it's the luck of the draw." Without a flash or special lenses, she learned as she went, making up for her lack of precision by taking three times the number of photographs an experienced photographer would.

By the time she was 37, Eleanor needed a break from the emotional demands of nursing. For a year, she traveled throughout the United States with her camera at her side. "About halfway through my travels, I was buying postcards of the Grand Canyon to send to my friends and family and I thought, 'I have pictures like these. I have pictures that are *better* than these.'"

When she returned home, the seed of an idea planted at the Grand Canyon—to publish her own line of photograph cards—blossomed into an obsession. "I wanted to do something to keep the photography alive after I started back into nursing. I was afraid that if I didn't make some kind of statement, the camera was just going to go back in the closet, and I was going to get wrapped up in nursing again," she says.

# Part-Time Careers

Although Eleanor's initial research revealed that her prospective business venture might be an "expensive statement," she proceeded to set up a company called "Just for You." Initially, she made the rounds of card and bookstores and gift shops with 25 of her own photographs pasted on good card stock. Again, she was learning as she went. "It was literally eight months from the time I started showing my cards to the time I took the final eight images to the publisher. I didn't have children, so I talked about my creative statement as 'my baby.' It seemed like I was birthing this project," she muses.

She worked nights as a nurse and marketed her cards during the day. Soon she was showing her work at local coffee houses and in galleries. "Once I identified myself as a photographer, other parts of the business just evolved," she says. Soon she was focusing exclusively on portraits of children and families and had cut her nursing down to three or four nights a week so she could expand her photography business.

"The people who hired me were interested in recording their kids, not as pretty little objects, but as a six-month-old or a three-year-old. They started having me photograph the children regularly. I have been photographing the majority of families I work with today for at least five years, and some for eight or ten years. I'm very interested in the whole generative process. Photography has allowed that to happen."

But there is at least one more snapshot. "I'm planning to take an early retirement from nursing and move to Oregon. People ask if I'm going to continue my photography there, and I say, 'maybe.' I see that part of my life as another chapter. There are two things very important to me: freedom and flexibility. I'm always staying open."

Back when she returned from her cross-country sabbatical, Eleanor's main goal was to try to establish a photography business. "Nursing was going to be a means to let that happen. I told myself that I could stand anything for a year. It's been 14 years. That's how well it's worked for me."

## At home, outside the norm

It is Tuesday afternoon. "We're going to the lumberyard to buy drywall," Bert Gilbert announces to his 2-year-old son, Keilor. Bert and a friend will spend the rest of the day hanging the walls in the downstairs bathroom.

That's how it's been going for the better part of six years as Bert has borrowed time from his work as a master carpenter to completely renovate the 130-year-old farmhouse he lives in with his wife, Amy, and their son.

"No one had lived in the upstairs for 40 years before we bought the house," he says. "We're gutting all the walls and putting in new insulation and wiring. We've also replaced the downstairs floors in three rooms." Over the course of the project, he is teaching himself everything he needs to know—from building codes to how to use the latest tools.

"Amy helps with the painting and I hire out maybe 5 percent of the work," he says. "But otherwise I do almost everything—the ceramic tile, plumbing, electrical. I had the heating/cooling guy come in and we designed the heating cooling system together."

With college degrees in sculpture, painting and business management, Bert was looking toward law school or a graduate degree in fine arts. "But when I thought about what I really wanted to do, I found myself doing more of this kind of stuff. I enjoy woodworking and I've always been kind of a handyman. Maybe it's not the kind of work you should do with a college education, but it's what I really love doing."

What may seem like a far cry from his original career path has, on closer inspection, an underlying logic of its own. "I think of my house as a sculpture right now," Bert says. The businessman in him is becoming a wise investor in real estate and farming. "We have 120 acres. We can cut hay off of it and raise a few head of cattle. In 10 more years, everything will be paid off."

# Part-Time Careers

Meanwhile, he says, "I think I'll probably get to the point where I work as a subcontractor and pick and choose jobs that I like to do on a part-time basis." I'd like to get my fine arts going again, so I plan to build a ceramic, sculpture and painting studio out back for myself, and a weaving studio for Amy."

He has a quiet confidence about the rewards of producing his living with his own hands. "When you're working with your hands, there's a physical reality when you're done with the job. It either works and looks good or it doesn't. In the corporate world there might be a little more room for things to get lost in the chain of command."

Creating a simpler, more self-sufficient lifestyle for his family gives him satisfaction and security that working in the corporate world never would have. "I think you have to remember that it's an awful short life to give it all away to your employer."

## An unmistakable sign

With a growing family to support, Renda Gauwitz grew accustomed to working behind a desk for eight hours a day, five days a week. She lived for the weekends, when she could ride and train her three horses.

But when a few people at her stables began to ask her for riding lessons, she sat down to do the math. "It was enough to pay for the care and board of my horses," she said. So she left her full-time job and went into partnership with a woman who had been her riding instructor. Together they trained horses and gave lessons in horseback riding and dressage.

"At the same time, word got out in the deaf community that I wasn't working full-time any more, and within two weeks of leaving my full-time job I started getting requests for my services as an interpreter," she says. The hearing child of two deaf parents, Renda has been fluent in American Sign Language since before she could talk. Over the years she'd filled in as an interpreter, off and on. So during that first year, she says, "I scheduled interpreting when I didn't have lessons."

But when it came time to prepare her income taxes, Renda was surprised to find the horseback riding lesson didn't pay off. "I was clearing maybe five dollars an hour," she says. There also was the nagging worry about the liability for accidents, even thought the teaching partnership was incorporated. But most of all, "I was tired," she admits. "Grooming and saddling the horses and giving the lessons is very, very physical work. Sometimes it was 100 degrees. Sometimes it was 10 below."

Suddenly the interpreting, something she had always taken for granted, took on a new appeal. "It made more sense to concentrate on interpreting. I was making from $15 to $30 an hour, plus mileage for travel over 20 miles one way. I could deduct any other mileage. I had no other expenses. I enjoyed it. I was good at it. And more and more people wanted me."

While there isn't a large deaf community in Peoria, Ill., where she lives, many of the available interpreters are not skilled in voicing what a deaf person is signing. "The deaf people were frustrated with the struggle just to be understood," Renda says. "I'm totally fluent, because it's my natural language. So I was always their first choice."

These days, her work runs the gamut from in-patient drug and alcohol abuse and family counseling to interpreting during workshop sessions at a national conference to voicing for contestants in the Miss Deaf Illinois Beauty Pageant. Many times she must act as both interpreter and advocate for pregnant women, accompanying them to doctor's visits, for sonograms and sometimes signing through the actual birth.

She also plans to teach part-time in Illinois Central College's newly established two-year associate program in interpreting.

With her children grown and on their own, Renda and her husband still support three horses. Even though her passion for riding no longer bears the burden of producing an income, it has been joined by another heartfelt pursuit—serving her extended family in the deaf community. "I'm from their world. I've found through the years that I really need to maintain that contact to feel like a whole person. I didn't always realize that," she admits.

## Too tall to live, too weird to die

When Amy Inouye rescued the 22-foot-tall statue with the body of a man and the head of a chicken from atop a downtown Los Angeles restaurant in 1984, she didn't envision a career in the mail-order business—much less in video, retail management or publishing. She had successfully run her own typesetting and graphic design studios for years without having to deal with bulk mail, sell stock or participate in high-level corporate negotiations.

At the time, she simply wanted to save another pop art landmark in danger of vanishing from the L.A. landscape. But like many simple beginnings, this small first act led to bigger things. In fact, for Amy, it has been something of an entrepreneurial and spiritual odyssey.

With Chicken Boy safely in storage, she approached a few museums and film production companies before "quite innocently" starting to produce Chicken Boy T-shirts, pens and other toys to give clients and friends. "A lot of my reason for my putting faith in Chicken Boy was because it was my way out of graphics," she admits. "I'm a graphic designer who is not completely in love with graphic design, which has been bad for my business. I like it a lot, but I don't love it."

Love has undoubtedly been behind the success of what she calls a "weird business that sells nothing that is vital to mankind." But even she was surprised by the effect the cult hero she has created has had on a growing number of fans across the country. "I know that Chicken Boy touches people's lives in a very positive fashion," she says, and can produce a fat file of letters and poems addressed to him as evidence.

Over the years, her love for her work has also made up for lack of cash, manpower and business acumen. Brochures were photocopied. Later, friendly printers agreed to charge only for materials and print the brochure in off-hours. Friends modeled clothing and jewelry and scouted new products. Amy herself has served as chief buyer, copywriter and order-filler.

Today the Chicken Boy catalog is mailed to more than 12,000 customers and prospects across the country—all referrals. Something of a cult-communique, it features 200 "very cool" gifts, from 3-D glasses for 85 cents to a lava light for $60, as well as the "True Story of Chicken Boy," whom Amy insists is "an inspiration to all the alternative lifestylists and urban pop aficionados."

But the appeal of the chicken that was "too tall to live, too weird to die," promises to reach far beyond the mail-order business. One Ohio fan, a professional video producer, has already written and produced "Chicken Boy: The Movie." It premiered at off-beat party-events in L.A. and San Francisco and was recently accepted as one of the half-hour segments to be aired in a 26-week series featuring independently produced comedy films on the Learning Channel. After that it will move to the Public Broadcasting Service (PBS).

Amy was tapped to open a retail store at a new mall called City Walk, right outside Universal Studio and can already see the day when Chicken Boy will be moved from storage to the plaza near the mall. She and a manager will handle retail sales 12 hours a day, seven days a week from a freestanding kiosk. "For six months, I'll be running back and forth and working a few hours a night. I'll still squeeze in the graphics whenever I can."

A publishing project may bring the business full circle. Amy plans to write what she jokingly calls a "how-not-to-run-a-business book" that will humorously chronicle the illogical growth of a business that she insists was never run as a business.

# Part-Time Careers

"I really always felt that it was going to pay off eventually. As it unfolds, it all seems to me like I just sort of hitched my cart onto this dream and it's taking me now."

## Just sing

"When I was young I was always singing, always performing for neighbors. So, as I grew up, I figured that's what I should do," says Steve Stevens.

But even with classical training in voice/performance from a top-notch university, he returned to his home in Seattle and "just kind of floundered." He sang a little and tried teaching. "But I wasn't quite sure what I wanted to do."

A year and half working for his father in the floor covering business was enough to focus his goals. He jumped at an opportunity to move to San Francisco where he planned to resume his singing, find an agent and then set his sights on graduate school.

With a stable income from waiting tables at a fifties-style restaurant, Steve is using his free time to establish himself as a voice instructor. He plans to use student fees to pay for his own voice training as he applies for scholarships to graduate programs in performance. In the not-too-distant future, he can see himself writing and performing as part of a University faculty, or studying and performing abroad as a Fulbright scholar.

"I want to get good at as many things as possible so I can be innovative."

Yet he is practical about waiting tables in the meantime. "I was going to phase out my job as a waiter," he admits. "I wasn't doing well at work because my mind was on other things. But I realized that, if I'm ever in a bind, even overseas, I would be able to pick up shifts, maybe even become a manager. So, I've decided to turn that up a notch even while I'm going after my goals."

And at 27, he is serious about making up for lost time. "I'm pretty driven. But I also had to make sure I was doing what I'm doing for the right reasons. When I initially started, I just wanted to be famous. That doesn't last for very long, or take you very far. Now that I'm going after my dream, I feel like I'm gaining ground every day. I feel more on top of things, more focused about everything, really."

## Unfinished stories

In these half-dozen stories are the seeds of inspiration. But if you've just embraced your own passion, how will you take those first steps toward your own dream? How will you deal with finances and manage changing relationships? Like these role models, you'll have to figure it out as you go along. But they can offer some concrete support by their own examples. Read on.

# Chapter 14

# Tapping your passion

"You have to get to a point where there's no distinction between your life and your work," says Amy Inouye. "If you know what you need to do to have that quality of life, you just do it."

Sage advice. Whether you are single or married, living in a big city or a suburban neighborhood, if you're pursuing your life's passion, you have every right to feel blessed.

Undoubtedly, you also will feel burdened. Sometimes it may seem as if you are defining your life by the sacrifices you make. The financial uncertainty. The odd hours. But these are merely threads woven into a larger pattern. What sometimes seems like a crazy quilt is, in fact, a life-in-progress—its logic becoming more exquisite with each passing milestone.

But once you shed the standard prescription for living your life, how will you know if you are doing it right?

You won't, until you look back to see how far you've come. Until then, you can find insight and inspiration in the experiences of others who are following similar paths.

## Flexible hours: Getting time on your side

If you're pursuing a passion, you already know time can be more precious than money. Many talk of stealing time in pieces of days and weeks, or hoarding chunks of time as if they were precious jewels.

Although many modern writers might yearn to steal away to the solitude of the legendary garret, modern times call for more realistic measures.

"When I started writing the first draft of my novel, each chapter was coming out very quickly, in about four hours. So spending part of each day at work and the rest of the day writing worked out well," says Tracy Fetters.

Her dilemma? "Now that I've written about half of the book, it's taking on momentum, building toward the climax." Because her schedule as a part-time editor tends to be very heavy during the final stages of the magazine's production cycle each month, she was able to negotiate a full-time schedule during the two busiest weeks of the month so she would be able to take the following two weeks off to finish the first draft.

"Ideally, I'd like to then go back to work full-time for two or three weeks or a month so I could take off another chunk of time to revise it."

"Working the graveyard shift was the only way I could do it," says Eleanor Bissell of balancing the emotional demands of nursing and the business of photography. "Working three nights a week nursing was the best balance. I had enough energy to expand my photography business." But when hospital needs changed, she had to take on an additional night. "On this schedule, I do tend to get tired and have a few days where I'm brain dead."

Working a set schedule each week is the key to her success. From Friday evening until Tuesday morning, she works as a nurse, sleeping the first four hours after she returns home and the last four hours before she goes to work. She uses the remaining part of those days to return telephone calls, set appointments for portrait sittings, show her work to prospective clients and run to the printer. Wednesday, Thursday and Friday of each week are devoted to photography.

## Living with your work

As one of the master carpenters for a local contracting firm, Bert Gilbert has been able to work out two scheduling options. Sometimes he must work full-time to complete a job, so he takes several weeks off afterward. Other times, he works three 10-hour days a week and uses his days off to work on his own home.

If that sounds like "the life," he is quick to point out that long days and a long commute between job sites and his rural home outside of Bloomington, Ind., often place him and his wife on the same time-treadmill many full-time, two-income couples face. "By the time we feed our son and give him a bath, it's 8:30 and we're thinking, 'Gosh, maybe we'll make something for *our* dinner tonight.'"

Add to that the stress of coming home to a house that has been under renovation for the past six years. "You're always at work," he says. "It's tough trying to do this part-time because so many jobs are interrelated. For example, you can't work in the bedroom when you're putting in plumbing for two new bathrooms." As a result, each project seems never-ending and requires an extra measure of patience.

Current low interest rates have prompted Bert and his wife to talk of taking out a loan so that he can take two or three months off to finish the rest of the work.

## Relationships: Bending the ties that bind

No man—or woman—is an island. Family, friends, lovers and children all are affected by the choices you'll make and the risks you'll take to pursue your goals. While there are some pleasant surprises, there are many more long-term public relations campaigns waged. Typically these struggles only strengthen your resolve.

"When I was still in Seattle, I didn't get to see anybody while I was focused on singing. I think that's part of the reason I stopped for a while," admits Steve Stevens. When he moved to San Francisco, he decided to take a different approach. "I sold some things like my car, so I could spend about a month building friendships without having to worry about getting right into the grind. Now, I'm beginning to establish relationships with people in my field. But my schedule still distances me from most of the people I know who work full-time."

"Remodeling is one of the most stressful things you can do to a marriage, outside of divorce," laughs Bert Gilbert. That the only working bathroom in his home happens to be at the end of an attached breezeway 30 feet behind the house, while the bedroom is on the front of the house on the second floor attests to the strength of his commitment. In addition, there are the wiles of a 2-year-old to contend with. "I spend half the time trying to placate my son while trying to get things done."

For many couples, fluctuating finances can be an issue. At least in the beginning. "It was hard for my husband to accept the fact that we never knew how much money we were going to have each month," admits Renda Gauwitz. Like many entrepreneurs, she must sometimes juggle funds to ease the cash flow clogs. "It's still hard, but we've managed. When we need to juggle, we juggle. And when I've gotten five checks in a row, I catch up on things. He's still a bit uptight, but it's not a problem in our relationship.

## Finances: Taking the taskmaster to task

You will probably define wealth in terms of the quality of the life you are creating. But at some point, you must make your peace with money. Or it will become a stern taskmaster.

# Part-Time Careers

You may be making a bundle, but your cash flow is only be as fluid as your clients. "The State of Illinois is my biggest employer. They are also broke," says Renda Gauwitz. "Sometimes I don't get paid for a job for six or seven months. I may bill $2,500 one month and be poor. It just shows up one day."

Soon she expects to be teaching part-time at a local community college. "That means locking myself into a regular schedule, but I'll still be able to accept freelance jobs and I'll have a regular income every month." She adds, "Then, everyone will be happy."

"Photography has supported itself, but not me," Eleanor Bissell says. "It covers expenses and allows some savings. But I needed to keep it a pleasurable thing. To put the burden on photography to support me would have changed my relationship with it. Now I can work with the people I want to work with. I don't feel like I'm grubbing for money."

Although nursing was once a vehicle to buy more time for photography, she finds her goals have shifted in recent years. "I can see my way clear to an early retirement. Now I don't mind putting in more hours at the hospital and maxing out on the savings, knowing that in four years I'll be having so much more freedom, so much more time."

"If you become 'known,' everybody assumes that you're really doing well and really you're just plugging along, pursuing your vision," observes Amy Inouye. Although she has achieved some national notoriety among fans of her mail-order cult figure, Chicken Boy, "I'm in debt to a certain degree. But that's not stopping me, because I'm compulsive about doing what I'm doing. I'm figuring out some way to do it, and finding people to give me credit."

## Consulting your own wisdom

"The few times I've gone out and hired consultants to help me with something, such as doing my mailing list or making my catalog better, I didn't find them to be that helpful," admits

Amy Inouye. "It was nice to be able to talk to somebody. But, you know, if I sat down and thought about the same problems or had my friends over to dinner and made them talk about them, we would come up with maybe even better solutions. As I get bigger, that may change. But those experiences have helped me realize that I can handle a lot more things myself."

## Strategies: How to manage your life's passion

If you've just starting out, be bold, but begin small. Here are nine guidelines to help you chart your unique path.

**1. Appreciate the power of solitude.** It is an essential attribute in anyone wishing to create a singular life—and a necessary ingredient in realizing your goals. As keeper of the talent that drives your passion, you may already realize you do your best work alone.

So, make quiet time a regular ritual. Take time to observe your work patterns. Are you a morning person or night person? What are your rhythms through the day and week? Do you require frequent breaks? Do you do your best work at a furious pace before a deadline? How can you continue to refresh your creative reserves and protect yourself from the stress of blows to your bank book or your ego?

"The best—and worst—thing about what I'm doing is that I'm all alone," says Tracy Fetters. "Sometimes I feel 'stuck' with this. But there aren't that many people stuck with the imagination and ability to tell stories. These fictitious places and people and things that happen are all in my mind. It's all within me. It's the most satisfying thing there is to create this world and be able to tell it to other people."

As you continue to keep private counsel, you will see how you're doing and whether you should change direction or tactics.

"During my very busy season, October through December, I get pretty crazed," says Eleanor Bissell. "I can get very jazzed up by people wanting my work. But there's another part of me that wants to be quiet, and read and write. That's the part of me I have to keep sacred and not let the business demands overwhelm me."

**2. Give yourself permission to try.** Some of your friends are telling you to "Go for it!"—even in the face of overwhelming odds. Acquaintances and family members may be counting down all the reasons it "will never work."

For now, turn a deaf ear to the nay-sayers and do your own research. Many people who pursue a life's passion do so in the face of overwhelming odds. Most lack a formal education or skills or clients. Knowing the areas in which you are lacking knowledge or support will help you seek out what you need. People whose values and opinions you trust and respect—mentors or associates who believe in you and will tell you the truth—can also be a boon.

When the idea for her current novel-in-progress wouldn't leave her alone, Tracy Fetters enrolled in a novel-writing workshop through *Writer's Digest* magazine. "I needed someone to hold my hand through the first 50 pages," she says. "My mentor wasn't a friend or part of the family. She was a published novelist who could give me objective advice and criticism. The first time she saw a chunk of my book, she said, 'I don't know when I've seen a better manuscript. You have the feel of a successful writer. When you finish this book, send it out. If it comes back, which I doubt, don't revise it. Start working on your next one.' "

**3. Create a network.** Reach out—whether you become active in a professional organization, establish a loose social-professional confederation of passion-seekers or simply lunch often with an informal "business buddy" you can trust as a sounding board. Other people can provide you with valuable information, leads and contacts. They can console you when the chips are down and be your lifeline when your business threatens to overwhelm you.

As an experienced entrepreneur, Amy Inouye knows, "You have to know when to ask for help. Your whole support structure—from your personal life to your vendors—has to be reliable. L.A. is a magnet for people who are willing to follow their dreams. We're aware of each other's existence and when we're around each other we talk about how hard it is and how things should be happening for all of us. Once you find people in the same boat and start opening up to them about your problems, you find that even people you assume are more 'together' than you are, aren't necessarily. That helps."

Sometimes a telephone call to a stranger is all it takes. "I remember feeling devastated by a client who wanted to pay less than I was charging—and I was already charging too little," Eleanor Bissell says. "I looked in the phone book and called a photographer I had never met for advice. It turned out that part of his career was teaching people how to market themselves.

"He spent 15 minutes on the phone with me telling me he could give me a formula for pricing, but that was only going to put a value on the material, not on the talent. He told me that first I had to value my work. At a time I was feeling undervalued by a client, this person I didn't even know was giving me a pep talk. That's typical of the kinds of feedback I have gotten."

**4. Teach yourself what you need to know.** A college degree is not always essential. In fact, many people pursuing a passion will tell you they distrust anything but their own experience. They are more willing to use a little chutzpah, to learn by the seat of their pants.

So read and observe. Cultivate your good resources. Surround yourself with people you respect, who know what you need to know and are willing to guide you. Every time you see an improvement, renew your efforts. Your curiosity will drive you to seek out the information needed. Your drive will give you wings.

"When I first started out, I needed work so badly I just said 'OK, I can do this,' and then went to the library and checked out every book on the subject," Bert Gilbert admits. "I still read a lot of publications and books. You learn a lot better that way. You might be able to learn some tricks from a co-worker, but a lot of tradespeople don't really love what they're doing, so they're not the best teachers. There are not a lot of people around who can handle the diversity of things I can, so that gives me a lot of flexibility."

"When I photographed my first two weddings for fellow nurses, they knew that my best feature was candids," says Eleanor Bissell. "They had to understand that, or I wasn't comfortable. I used to take about three times the number of pictures a normal photographer would because I didn't want to miss anything. Then, when I'd get something back from the printer that I didn't quite understand, he would talk to me about it and give me suggestions."

Amy Inouye continues to learn by example, inspiration and the occasional error as she runs her mail-order business, and delves into the worlds of retail, video and publishing. She's philosophical about her mistakes. "It's self-education, I guess. You experiment and figure out what you can and cannot do. It hasn't been a loss. I've been paying to learn what I've learned."

**5. Experiment with lifestyle schedules.** Will you work nights? Part of every day? Or an intense few weeks so that you can take the next few weeks off? Much depends on your internal "time clock" and the demands your passion makes on your time and energy.

But, rest assured. There are almost as many possibilities as people. Although it's unrealistic to expect employers to give you *carte blanche* in molding your working hours to the requirements of your outside interests, you may be surprised at the flexibility possible. In many cases, it depends on the job, the industry and your own initiative.

"If I feel like working until midnight, I work until midnight," Amy Inouye declares. "If I feel like going to a movie at 3 in the afternoon and the decks are clear, I don't feel guilty about doing that, because I know I make up for it in other ways. The whole flow of my life is OK. My life, my work, it's all the same. The key is to not let it get overwhelming. When it gets overwhelming, you have to start letting go of whatever it is you can."

**6. Rediscover how much—or how little—money you require.** Money can seem like an uncompromising taskmaster. But when you step back from social standards and look for ways to scale back your lifestyle, you may be surprised to find how many unnecessary "extras" you can comfortably eliminate. In fact, you may find you have unknowingly created the whip you have been using to drive your full-time workstyle.

"After college, I worked as a waiter for a year to think about what I wanted to do and to see how little money I would need to live on and still be happy," remembers Bert Gilbert. "I found out I don't need a whole lot. And when you don't need a whole lot of money, your choices can be based on a lot of other things. When money is not your goal, it frees you."

**7. Don't become invested in false starts.** "I left law school three times," admits Tracy Fetters. "That may have set a record at the University of Virginia. The first time, I was there for two weeks. When I went back the next year, I started dropping classes. I was very unhappy. I was taking the necessary steps to be a lawyer, but it felt so wrong."

Halfway through her third year, she developed acute carpal tunnel syndrome (a painful constriction of the nerves in the wrist, usually caused by excessive typing or handwriting.) It was a reason to drop out for good. "I didn't know what I was going to do," she says. But, while working as a bartender, she got the idea for her novel, currently in progress.

**8. Relax and let it evolve.** Not conventional wisdom in the working world. And difficult to do. When you're not sure of the next bend in the road, you will need to live by your wits and trust your experience and intuition to guide you.

"The thing that has amazed me is how the business has evolved by my just trusting timing and my intuition," says Eleanor Bissell. "You can set things in motion, but you shouldn't feel like you have to control the outcome. You have to let something have its life and trust that it's OK to give yourself the permission to let that happen."

**9. When the going gets tough, persist.** According to the dictionary, passion is both "boundless enthusiasm," as well as the object of that enthusiasm. It is the distinguishing characteristic that drives someone to go on in the face of financial difficulties and uncertain success.

"Having had one career already that was very unsatisfying, I feel fortunate that in my late 20s and early 30s, I found something that is right for me," says Tracy Fetters. She is the first to tell you she has met with more than her share of obstacles in the path to finishing her novel. But even so, "I will do whatever it takes and make whatever sacrifices I need to make to continue pursuing it."

# Epilogue

*"The great French Marshall Lyautey once asked his gardener to plant a tree. The gardener objected that the tree was slow-growing and would not reach maturity for 100 years. The Marshall replied, 'In that case, there is no time to lose. Plant it this afternoon.'"*
—John F. Kennedy

Your career is like a slow-growing tree—the shape it takes is up to you. Neglect the root system and the entire tree will weaken. Let the branches go wild and the growth will be random and uneven.

By "pruning" hours from your full-time schedule to create a part-time or flexible workstyle, you will nourish the roots of your personal life and strengthen the branches of your professional life. Your growth will be more substantial, and the shape of your progress more defined.

With courage and persistence, you will learn from your mistakes—growth is forgiving. With planning, you will always be able to keep your priorities in balance. By standing apart from the rest of the forest, you will develop a talent for reaching out, and up, in new directions.

With the care of a gardener and the vision of a leader, you can create a satisfying workstyle that works over the many seasons of your life.

Start today. It will not take 100 years.

# Resources

## National organizations and associations

### Association of Part-Time Professionals
7700 Leesburg Pike, Suite 216
Falls Church, VA 22043
(703) 734-7975

Established in 1978 to promote part-time employment at the professional level, this national, nonprofit organization is an authority on flexible work options. It provides information, resources and job referrals on flexible work arrangements to members. Publishes *Working Options*. Offices in Washington, D.C., Boston, Philadelphia and Hampton, NH.

### Clearinghouse on Work and Family
Women's Bureau
U.S. Department of Labor
200 Constitution Avenue, N.W.
Washington, DC 20210
(202) 219-4486
Provides research on work and family issues.

### Bureau of National Affairs
1231 25th Street NW
Washington, DC 20037
(800) 372-1033 or (202) 452-4200

This private publisher provides specialized information on employee relations, environment and safety, law, taxation, business and economics. Special report series on work and family and hosts an annual conference.

### Catalyst
250 Park Avenue South
5th Floor
New York, NY 10003-1459
(212) 777-8900

This nonprofit organization primarily works with businesses to effect change for women through research, advisory services and communications. An extensive publications list includes in-depth information about flexible work arrangements, as well as career development resources.

**Conference Board, Inc.**
Work and Family Information Center, 845 Third Avenue
New York, NY 10022
(212) 759-0900

Provides information to senior executives on work and family related issues.

**Families and Work Institute**
330 Seventh Avenue
New York, NY 10001
(212) 465-2044

Focusing on policy research and corporate strategic planning, this organization serves as a national clearinghouse for information on work/family issues and develops training programs and educational materials for clients in government and business. Publishes *Corporate Reference Guide*, outlining work/family policies and programs at some 200 U.S. corporations.

**Family Resource Coalition**
200 So. Michigan Ave., Ste. 1520
Chicago, IL 60604
(312) 341-0900

With more than 2,000 individuals and organizations as members, this organization produces numerous publications including work/family program resource kits for employers.

**Family Service America**
11700 West Lake Park Drive
Park Place
Milwaukee, WI 53224
(414) 359-1040

Provides referrals nationwide to individuals seeking work/family counseling.

**New Ways to Work**
149 Ninth Street
San Francisco, CA 94103
(415) 552-1000

This work resource center conducts research, serves as a clearinghouse for information on alternative work arrangements and promotes flexible work arrangements. Publishes *Work Times*, quarterly.

**9 to 5**
National Association of Working Women
614 Superior Avenue NW
Cleveland, OH 44113
(216) 566-9308

This membership organization for office workers operates a Job Survival Hotline 1-800-522-0925. Trained job counselors respond to questions about flexible jobs, maternity leave and balancing work and family, between 10 a.m. and 4:30 p.m.

## Career Counseling

(Look in your local yellow pages for counselors/consultants specializing in "alternative" or "flexible work schedules.")

# Part-Time Careers

## Books on flexible work options in companies

*The Best Jobs in America for Parents, Who Want Careers and Time for Children Too.* Susan Bacon Dynerman and Lynn O'Rourke Hayes, Ballantine Books.

*Getting to Yes, Negotiating Agreement Without Giving In.* Roger Fisher and William Ury, Harvard Negotiation Project, Houghton Mifflin Co.

*The Job Sharing Handbook.* Barney Olmstead and Suzanne Smith, Ten Speed Press.

*The Part-Time Solution.* Charlene Canape, Harper & Row, Publishers.

*Temp By Choice.* Diane Thrailkill, Career Press.

*What Color is Your Parachute? A Practical Manual for Job-hunters and Career Changers.* Richard Nelson Bolles, Ten Speed Press.

*You Can Negotiate Anything.* Herb Cohen, Bantam Books.

## Resources for home-based business owners and telecommuters

**Mothers' Home Business Network**
P.O. Box 423
East Meadow, NY 11554
(516) 997-7394
   Publishes *Homeworking Mothers* newsletter.

**National Association for the Cottage Industry**
P.O. Box 14850
Chicago, IL 60614
(312) 472-8116
   Publishes *The Cottage Connection* and *The Kern Report* with news of trends and issues of interest to home-based business owners and telecommuters.

**National Association of Home-based Businesses**
P.O. Box 30220
Baltimore, MD 21270
(410) 363-3698
   Publishes home-based business newspaper.

**Small Business Administration (SBA)**
409 Third Street SW
Washington, DC 20416
(800) 827-5722
   The primary source of federal assistance for small businesses. Offers loans, order free publications, workshops and benefit from

management assistance and counseling. For the SBA office closest to you, refer to the blue government pages of your phone book, or call 800-UASK-SBA.

**Answer Desk Hotline**
(800) 827-5722. Offers details on resources and recorded information on many topics.

**Small Business Development Centers (SBDCs).** With about 700 locations on college campuses in all 50 states, this is a resource for counseling on the financial, marketing and technical areas of your new business.

**Small Business Institutes (SBIs).** Located on some 500 university and college campuses, these centers are staffed by a senior business administrator and marketing students who offer free guidance.

**SCORE (Service Corps of Retired Executives).** This network of 13,000 retired business executives and professionals offers volunteer services to help small business people on the spot or on an indefinite basis. Low-cost business management seminars are available.

# Books on starting/running a home-based business

*Best Home Businesses for the '90s.* Paul and Sarah Edwards, Jeremy P. Tarcher, Inc.

*The Complete Work-At-Home Companion, Everything You Need to Know to Prosper as a Home-based Entrepreneur or Employee.* Herman Holtz, Prima Publishing & Communications.

*Retiring to Your Own Business.* Gustav Berle, Ph.D., Puma Publishing.

*Free Help From Uncle Sam to Start Your Own Business (Or Expand the One You Have).* William Alarid and Gustav Berle, Puma Publishing.

*Homemade Money: The Definitive Guide to Success in a Homebased Business.* Barbara Brabec, Betterway Publications, Inc.

*Working From Home: Everything You Need to Know About Living and Working Under the Same Roof.* Sarah and Paul Edwards, Jeremy P. Tarcher, Inc.

*How to Set Your Fees and Get Them.* Kate Kelly, Visibility Enterprises.

*The One-Minute Commuter, How to Keep Your Job and Stay at Home Telecommuting.* Lis Fleming, Acacia Books.

# Part-Time Careers

*The Telecommuter's Handbook, How to Work for a Salary— Without Ever Leaving the House.* Brad Schepp, Pharos Books, Scripps Howard Co.

*Making It on Your Own: Surviving and Thriving on the Ups and Downs of Being Your Own Boss.* Sarah and Paul Edwards, Jeremy P. Tarcher, Inc.

*Small Time Operator: How to Start Your Own Business, Keep Your Books, Pay Your Taxes and Stay Out of Trouble.* Bernard Kamoroff, CPA, Bell Springs Publishing.

## Temporary placement firms for professionals

Here are a few agencies that specialize in placing management-level professionals in temporary positions. Look in the yellow pages for agencies in your area.

**Accountemps/Robert Half International**
2884 Sandhill Rd., Suite 200
Menlo Park, CA 94025
(415) 854-9700
Places accountants from offices nationwide.

**The Experts**
3 Newton Executive Park
Newton, MA 02162
(617) 527-4500
Places computer consultants, including project leaders, trainers, technical writers and business analysts.

**Freelancers Over 50**
99 First Street
Cambridge, MA 02141
(617) 354-4102

**CompHealth/KRON**
Group One
4021 South 700 East
Salt Lake City, UT 84107
(800) 453-3030
Places doctors and allied health professionals.

**The Lawsmiths**
2443 Fillmore Street, #319
San Francisco, CA 94115
(415) 929-1090

**Lawyer's Lawyer**
1725 K Street NW, Suite 907
Washington, DC 20006
(202) 362-3333
    Places attorneys.

**Of Counsel, Inc.**
4149 Pennsylvania, Suite 306
Kansas City, MO 64111
(816) 753-4644
    Places paralegals and lawyers.

*The following agencies place management-level temporaries.*

**Klivans, Becker & Smith**
720 Hanna Building
1422 Euclid Avenue
Cleveland, OH 44115
(216) 621-2970

**Management Assistance
Group**
10 N. Main Street
West Hartford, CT 06107
(203) 523-0000

**Interim Management Corp.**
475 Park Ave. So., 33rd Floor
New York, NY 10016
(212) 213-3600

**The Corporate Staff**
177 Bovet Road
San Mateo, CA 94402
(415) 344-2613

# Index

# Part-Time Careers

# Part-Time Careers